SPECIAL NEEDS IN ORDINARY S

General editor: Peter Mittler

Associate editors: Mel Ainscow, Brahm Norwich, Peter Pumfrey, Rosemary Webb, Sheila Wolfendale

Honorary advisory board: Neville Bennett, Marion Blythman, George Cooke, John Fish, Ken Jones, Sylvia Phillips, Klaus Wedell, Philip Williams

Titles in the Special Needs in Ordinary Schools series

Meeting Special Needs in Ordinary Schools: An Overview (2nd edition)

Assessing Special Educational Needs
Management for Special Needs
Reappraising Special Needs Education

Concerning pre- and primary schooling:

Primary Schools and Special Needs: Policy, Planning and Provision (2nd edition)

Pre-School Provision for Children with Special Needs

Encouraging Expression: The Arts in the Primary Curriculum
Improving Children's Reading in the Junior School: Challenges and Responses

Concerning secondary schooling:

Secondary Schools for All? Strategies for Special Needs (2nd edition)

Humanities for All: Teaching Humanities in the Secondary School
Responding to Adolescent Needs: A Pastoral Care Approach
Science for All: Teaching Science in the Secondary School
Secondary Mathematics and Special Educational Needs
Shut Up! Communication in the Secondary School

Concerning specific difficulties:

Children with Hearing Difficulties
Children with Learning Difficulties
Children with Speech and Learning Difficulties
Improving Classroom Behaviour: New Directions for Teachers and Pupils
Mobility for Special Needs
Working with Parents of Children with Special Needs

Forthcoming:

Educating the Able
Further Opportunities: Learning Difficulties and Disabilities in Further Education

Working with Parents of Children with Special Needs

Garry Hornby

CASSELL

Cassell
Wellington House
125 Strand
London WC2R 0BB

215 Park Avenue South
New York
NY 10003

British Library Cataloguing-in-Publication Data
A catalogue record for this book is available from the British Library.

ISBN   0-304-32859-6 (hardback)
        0-304-32857-X (paperback)

Typeset by York House Typographic Ltd.
Printed and bound in Great Britain by Biddles Ltd,
Guildford and King's Lynn

Contents

Editorial foreword   vii

Dedication and Acknowledgements   ix

Introduction   x

1 Rationale for working with parents   1
Introduction   1
Professional attitudes towards parents   4
Attitudes needed to work effectively with parents   7
Knowledge needed to work effectively with parents   8
Skills needed to work effectively with parents   9
Parental rights in education   9
Parental roles in education   12
Summary and conclusions   15

2 Model for parent involvement   17
Introduction   17
Approaches to parent–professional relationships   18
The need for a model of parent involvement   22
Model for parent involvement   23
Using the model to guide parent involvement practice   29
Summary and conclusions   34

3 Understanding parents' reactions and needs   35
Introduction   35
Coming to terms with a child's special needs   36
Effects on and of family   43
Summary and conclusions   51

4 Helping parents of children with various special needs   53
Introduction   53
Children with disabilities   55
Children with medical conditions   61
Children coping with bereavement   66
Children coping with their parents' separation or divorce   79
Summary and conclusions   86

5 Interpersonal skills for working with parents 87
Introduction 87
Listening skills 88
Assertion skills 93
Counselling skills 100
Summary and conclusions 103

6 Communicating with parents 104
Introduction 104
Parent preferences 105
Informal contacts 106
Home visits 108
Telephone contacts 111
Written communication 113
Parent–teacher meetings 117
Summary and conclusions 123

7 Parental involvement in their children's education 125
Introduction 125
Effectiveness of parental involvement 127
Early intervention projects 128
Parent behavioural training 131
Parental involvement in reading 133
Parental involvement in other curriculum areas 138
Facilitating parental involvement in assessments
and reviews 139
Summary and conclusions 143

8 Working with parents in groups 144
Introduction 144
Benefits of group work with parents 145
Group leadership skills and knowledge 146
Parent education groups 149
Workshops for parents of children with special needs 153
Parent to Parent schemes 155
Other types of group work 157
Summary and conclusions 160

9 Working with parents: the future 161

Bibliography 163

Name index 173

Subject index 176

Editorial foreword

Although this book is published as a contribution to the *Special Needs in Ordinary Schools* series, its message is relevant to all children and all parents in every school. The time has come for the staff and governors of every school to review their home–school policy for all children and not just for those with special educational needs.

If education is concerned with everything which systematically helps children to learn and to develop, it follows that parents and teachers are natural partners. For the first five years, the parents and the family are the main educators; for the next eleven years at least, the task is shared to varying extent between families and teachers.

Good communication and effective collaboration with parents is one of the hallmarks of an effective school (National Commission on Education, 1993). Children whose parents are involved in their child's education and work with teachers to help their child learn and enjoy learning make better progress all round than those whose parents are less involved. This is true of all children but is particularly important where the child is experiencing difficulties, for any reason.

So much for the rhetoric. But we know that the reality is often very different. How often do we still hear a comment along the lines of 'What do you expect of a child from such a family?' This is a stereotyped judgement which should be regarded as unacceptable as a racist or sexist generalization. Similarly, it is not uncommon to hear teachers complain that certain parents are 'not interested in their child's education', giving as 'evidence' that they never come to parents' meetings.

Most teachers are committed to working collaboratively with parents and are constantly striving to find new ways of doing so. But there are obstacles. Very little time is devoted to working with parents either in the initial training of teachers or in post-experience in-service courses. Ask any large group of teachers how many have attended a course on parental involvement in the last year or even the last five years.

The government has not helped either. Using the politically correct language of parent choice and empowerment, they have in effect set up parents as teacher watchdogs – hardly a basis for partnership.

Several public opinion polls have shown beyond doubt that parents were in general solidly behind teachers in their protest about standard assessment tasks and strongly support schools in their struggle for more resources.

We need to find new ways of working with parents, particularly those who have in the past not shown much enthusiasm for working with schools. This book will help all schools to rethink their policies and practice, in the interests of the children they teach and the communities they serve.

Peter Mittler
University of Manchester
February 1995

REFERENCE

National Commission on Education (1993) *Learning to Succeed: A Radical Look at Education Today and a Strategy for the Future.* London: Heinemann.

Dedication

To my father, for setting me a superb example
and
to my mother, for always believing in me 100 per cent.

Acknowledgements

I would like to thank all the colleagues and parents, too numerous to mention, who I have worked with over the years, many of whom have contributed to the ideas presented in this book.

I would also like to thank Professor Peter Mittler and Professor Sheila Wolfendale for their helpful comments on an earlier draft of the book.

Finally, I would like to thank Naomi Roth and Justine White of Cassell for their support throughout the publication process.

Introduction

As many more children with special needs of various kinds are being educated in mainstream schools it is essential that their teachers develop the competencies necessary to work effectively with their parents. Establishing constructive working relationships with parents is a key element of meeting the educational needs of all children but it is particularly important for those children with special needs.

There are two main reasons for this. First, parents of children with special needs are likely to require greater support and guidance than many other parents. They may need help in coming to terms with their child's difficulties or seek guidance in coping with the child's behaviour at home. Second, there are many ways in which parents can help teachers to provide the most effective education for children with special needs. For example, they can supply valuable information about their children and reinforce at home what is learned at school.

After working with parents of children with special needs as a mainstream and special class teacher, educational psychologist and researcher as well as training teachers to work with parents as a lecturer in higher education, I have come to believe that developing collaborative working relationships with parents is the key to providing the most appropriate education for these children. I now consider that possessing the interpersonal skills, attitudes and knowledge needed for working effectively with parents is every bit as important as having the specific expertise necessary for teaching their children with special needs.

This book is aimed at helping teachers to work effectively with parents of children who have special needs of various kinds. The main types of special needs which teachers will be aware of are associated with various degrees of learning difficulty from dyslexia to profound intellectual disability, physical disabilities such as cerebral palsy and sensory losses such as hearing impairment. However, children with medical conditions such as asthma or cystic fibrosis are also likely to have special needs. In addition, problems resulting from the separation or divorce of their parents or the death of a close family member can also lead to children having special needs.

In this book, the term 'special educational needs' is used to refer to children with learning difficulties and to those with sensory or physical disabilities, as well as to children who have emotional or behavioural problems. Whereas, the term 'special needs' is used more broadly to refer also to a variety of other difficulties experienced by children, including those associated with chronic or life-threatening illnesses and the effects of losses such as bereavement and divorce. In fact, if the special needs associated with each of these difficulties are not adequately met then the children concerned are likely to develop learning difficulties or emotional or behavioural problems. That is, they will be at risk of developing special educational needs.

This book is intended to provide guidelines to teachers to help them improve their understanding of and working relationships with parents in order to facilitate the healthy development of all children who have special needs of any kind.

The first chapter provides a rationale for establishing effective working relationships with parents and outlines the attitudes, skills and knowledge which teachers need to develop. Chapter 2 discusses various approaches to working with parents and presents a model to guide professional practice which addresses parents' needs and also parents' strengths relevant to their involvement in their children's education. A check-list of aspects of parent involvement which need to be addressed in designing policy and procedures for working with parents is considered. Chapter 3 considers the process which parents and other family members go through in adapting to the knowledge that a child has a disability, medical condition or emotional and behavioural difficulties. Also discussed is how children with special needs are affected by their families and the wider environment in which they live.

Chapter 4 addresses the needs of parents of children with disabilities and other kinds of special needs, including those associated with health problems and those who have experienced a loss through bereavement or divorce. Chapter 5 outlines the interpersonal skills needed by teachers in order to work effectively with parents. These include listening skills, counselling skills and assertion skills. As such it is very much a 'how to' chapter focusing on skill development. Chapter 6 discusses the various methods of communicating with parents, such as home visits, parent–teacher meetings and different forms of written communication.

Chapter 7 considers the various forms of parental involvement in their children's education. This includes parental involvement in the assessment and statementing processes, home–school reading programmes and home–school behaviour programmes. Chapter 8 focuses on working with parents in groups such as in parent education programmes or parent to parent schemes. The organizational and group leadership skills needed by teachers in order to work with groups of parents are discussed. Finally, Chapter 9 comments on issues concerning the practice of parent involvement in the future such as the increased emphasis given to parent involvement in the 1993 Education Act and the general lack of training for teachers on working with parents.

Rationale for working with parents

INTRODUCTION

My first experience of the benefits of teachers working closely with parents happened when I was ten years of age. Around the age of seven I had developed a stammer which had got progressively worse. My parents had consulted the family doctor, who made a referral to a speech therapist. I went to speech therapy for about half a dozen sessions but it didn't seem to help. By the time I was in my final year at primary school my parents were quite concerned about the problem but were at a loss to know what else to try. Then, at a parents evening, my teacher suggested that elocution lessons would help and gave my parents the name of someone she recommended. As you can appreciate, as we lived in a working-class area of Rochdale, elocution lessons were not something which parents automatically considered for their children! Nevertheless, I started attending once a week and almost immediately the fluency of my speech improved. After a year my stammer was hardly noticeable and, in fact, I passed the grade one elocution examination with distinction! Though I stopped attending elocution after this, my stammer has remained under reasonable control ever since. I can still find certain words difficult if used to start sentences and sometimes feel uncomfortable using the telephone but I am now only aware of working hard to control my stammer when I get nervous in situations such as lecturing to very large groups of people.

The help my teacher gave to my parents has had a significant impact on my life. I would never have been able to work as a teacher, educational psychologist or university lecturer if I had not learned to control my stammer when I did. Not to mention the potentially devastating effect on my personal life which this difficulty with oral communication could have led to. So I am acutely aware of the debt I owe to this teacher, who had the interests of her pupils at heart and who used her knowledge of how my special need could be met and her interpersonal skills to persuade my parents to try something they would perhaps not have thought of themselves.

My professional interest in the benefits of teachers working closely with parents emerged when I was teaching adolescents with moderate learning difficulties in a secondary school special class in New Zealand twenty years ago. Several incidents highlighted the importance of having good working relationships with parents and stimulated my interest in learning more about this aspect of the teacher's role. Two incidents involving my pupils spring immediately to mind, one with which I had some success and one which left me feeling very frustrated.

First, there was Grant, who was 15 years old but had a reading age around 6 years and couldn't tell the time or handle money at all. On the first class outing into Auckland, for which the pupils caught buses from their homes into the centre of the city, Grant didn't turn up. When I visited him at home that evening his parents told me that he wasn't allowed to catch a bus by himself as they didn't think he could manage it. I then spent considerable time convincing Grant's parents that he needed to learn how to catch buses by himself and that he could learn to do so. After much discussion about Grant's difficulties and his future they agreed to let him catch the bus, under my supervision, the next time we had a class trip into Auckland.

After several rehearsals in class of what he needed to do, on the day of the next class trip Grant set out from home to catch the bus, with me watching him every step of the way. I watched him leave his house and walk to the bus stop, wait for the correct bus to come and then get on it and give the driver his fare. I then drove into the city centre to await the bus's arrival. When the bus pulled in and Grant climbed off, the look of accomplishment on his face suggested he'd done much more than simply catch his first bus. He beamed as if he'd just gone round the world by himself!

This was a big step for Grant but an even bigger one for his parents because it made them realize that he was ready to tackle quite grown-up things by himself. From then on I was able to work together with his parents to help Grant become as independent as possible. In fact, when he left school it was to start a job over the other side of the city from his home for which he had to change buses. But this was by then well within Grant's capacity.

The second incident involved Stephen who was also 15 but was more able than Grant and had a reading age of around 9 years. This incident occurred when Stephen's parents didn't turn up to a parent–teacher meeting. Since I was concerned about Stephen's somewhat bizarre behaviour at school I telephoned to suggest that, since I would pass their house on my way home from the meeting, if it was convenient, I could visit so that we could discuss his progress. This was agreed and I subsequently found myself deep in discussion with Stephen's parents about his childhood, his interests, his current behaviour and especially about what the aims of his educational programme should be. I found out that Stephen's father was very keen for him to learn maths and spent time each evening drilling him in such things as fractions and decimals. I tried to tactfully suggest that some of this work was too difficult for Stephen and that there were other more important things he could be learning. However, when I left the house, at one o'clock in the morning, his father's last words to me were 'There's a flagon of whisky in that cabinet and when Stephen passes his School Certificate maths it'll be opened'.

Needless to say, I found this very depressing. Stephen was as likely to pass this academic maths exam as he was to walk on water! But his father's comment had confirmed that I had not convinced him that there were a lot more useful things for Stephen to be learning. In fact I never did get through to his father and Stephen's behaviour continued to be somewhat bizarre. With hindsight, it seems that his father had difficulty in accepting Stephen's limitations which therefore made it impossible for him to plan appropriately for his future. The fact that I could make no impact on this situation made me feel very frustrated.

These and other similar incidents, which occurred while I was teaching the special class, highlighted for me the importance of parents in the development and education of their children with special needs. It was my successes in working with some of the parents which made me realize the potentially huge benefits to children of teachers working closely with their parents. But it was my inadequacy in situations like the one with Stephen's father which made me realize also that working effectively with parents was not easy and needed much more knowledge and skills than I had at that time.

These practical experiences gave me the incentive to learn more about working with parents. Over the past twenty years I have developed this interest and have worked with parents of children with special needs in numerous workshops and Parent to Parent training groups (see Chapter 8), in addition to working with parents as a teacher, educational psychologist, researcher and lecturer in special education. In recent years I have specialized in providing in-service training courses for teachers on working with parents. In this book I have drawn on the content of these courses in order to provide information which will help teachers develop the attitudes, knowledge and skills considered essential for working effectively with parents.

PROFESSIONAL ATTITUDES TOWARDS PARENTS

Research conducted with teachers in both special and mainstream schools indicates that they find interactions with parents to be a major source of stress in their jobs (Turnbull and Turnbull, 1986). On the other side of the fence, parents are reported to find communications with professionals such as teachers to be equally stressful. In fact, Sonnenschien (1984) has suggested that certain common attitudes which many professionals hold towards parents can contribute substantially towards this stress. These include the fact that parents are often viewed as being either problems or adversaries. Alternatively, they are seen as vulnerable, less able or in need of treatment themselves. In addition, parents are sometimes considered to be the cause of their children's problems. Finally, for various reasons, perhaps related to the above views, many professionals adopt an attitude of 'professional distance'. These common attitudes toward parents are discussed below, followed by discussion of attitudes which are more conducive to the development of effective working partnerships with parents.

Parents as problems

Some teachers see parents mainly as problems. When parents are convinced there is something wrong with their child despite reassurance from professionals, they are considered to be 'over-anxious'. When parents disagree with a diagnosis or the results of an assessment and ask for a second opinion they are said to be 'denying the reality' of the disability. When parents refuse to accept the educational programmes or placements suggested for their child, and are adamant about what they want, they are regarded as being 'aggressive'. Labelling parents in these ways tends to militate against the development of productive working relationships with them.

Parents as adversaries

There is a tendency for teachers to view parents as adversaries. Teachers may have different goals and priorities to parents for the educational programmes of the children that they teach. For example, in the incident discussed above, Stephen's father's priorities were very different from mine. This can create conflict and sometimes competition between parents and teachers. Competition can also be focused on children's achievements. Typically, children will behave more appropriately for their teachers than they will for their parents. In contrast, parents often report that children do things at home which are not observed at school. In these situations it is easy for either teachers or parents to feel doubtful or resentful about the others' success in getting the child to perform well. Avoiding the tendency to view parents as adversaries is essential for good relationships.

Parents as vulnerable

Teachers may regard parents as being too vulnerable to be treated as equal partners. This occurs most often when teachers are reluctant to tell parents the whole truth about their child's difficulties in case they become upset. So some of the child's weaknesses may be glossed over or parents may be given an overly optimistic view of their child's likely future progress. This does not promote the development of good relationships since parents are widely reported to appreciate professionals telling them all that they know about the child's difficulties as honestly as possible (see Chapter 3).

Alternatively, teachers who come across as superior will actually contribute to feelings of vulnerability in parents, which may lead to them becoming defensive and resistant to suggestions. Feeling vulnerable is an understandable reaction in parents who are seeking help for their child with special needs. Therefore, teachers should strive to allay this feeling, not add to it, as they sometimes unintentionally do, by developing the skills necessary for communicating sensitively and effectively with parents (as described in Chapter 5).

Parents as less able

There is a tendency for parents to be viewed as less observant, less perceptive and less intelligent than professionals. Therefore, parents' ideas and opinions are not given the credence which they deserve. This is a pity since most parents have an abundance of information about their children which can be invaluable to their teachers. A more helpful view is to consider that, while teachers are the experts on education, parents are the experts on their children.

Parents as needing treatment

Some professionals believe that having a child with special needs typically results in the parents developing personal problems and therefore being in need of counselling. This assumed pathology in parents then becomes the focus of professional attention. Such views are experienced as patronizing and extremely frustrating by parents. This is well illustrated by Roos (1978) who recounts that, despite holding a senior position in the disability field, his opinion was ignored and he was offered tranquillizers when he sought a diagnosis for his daughter's disability. It must be remembered that, while a minority of parents who have children with disabilities do benefit from personal counselling in order to help them cope with the situation, the majority of parents do not need it (Webster, 1977). In addition, some parents consider that they have become stronger as a result of the experience (Wikler *et al.*, 1983). It is therefore unwise to make assumptions about possible pathology in the parents. It is generally more helpful for the development of productive relationships when teachers focus on parents' strengths rather than any possible weaknesses.

Parents as causal

Another possible attitudinal barrier to developing effective working relationships with parents occurs when teachers consider that parents have caused or contributed to children's special needs. This tends to happen more with children who have emotional or behavioural difficulties. These are often considered by teachers to be caused by parents who have deprived their children of love or discipline. But even with children who have disabilities such as learning difficulties there is a tendency to assume that these have been made worse by poor parenting.

Many parents who have children with special needs experience guilt for one reason or another. Some wonder whether they are in any way responsible for causing the disability while others feel guilty about not being able to spend more time working with their children in order to overcome their difficulties. Therefore, it is of no benefit for professionals such as teachers to add to these guilt feelings by communicating to parents either indirectly or directly their views about the parents' role in causing their children's special needs.

Parents needing to be kept at a 'professional distance'

Many teachers prefer to keep parents at a professional distance. They don't want to establish close working relationships with parents in case this causes problems. This attitude can result from teachers subscribing to any of the negative attitudes discussed above or can be due to a lack of confidence about being able to relate well to parents. Also, the necessity for emotional distance to be maintained between professionals and their clients is an attitude which in the past has been encouraged on many professional training courses. Unfortunately, parents perceive this emotional distance as being indicative of the lack of empathy professionals have with their situation. They therefore typically have little confidence in any teachers who operate at such a distance.

ATTITUDES NEEDED TO WORK EFFECTIVELY WITH PARENTS

In contrast to the negative views of parents which are described above, the attitudes which teachers need in order to work effectively with parents are ones which will help them develop a productive partnership. To bring this about teachers need to communicate to parents the attitudes of *genuineness, respect* and *empathy* suggested by Carl Rogers (1980). They must be *genuine* in their relationships with parents. That is, they should come across as real people with their own strengths and weaknesses. For example, they should always be prepared to say that they 'don't know' when this is the case. Hiding behind a professional façade of competence is not in anyone's interest. Teachers also need to show *respect* for parents. Parents' opinions and requests should always be given the utmost consideration. In the final analysis parents' wishes should be respected even if they run counter to the views of teachers, since it is parents who have the long-term responsibility for their children. Most importantly, teachers need to develop *empathy* with parents. They should try to see the child's situation from the point of view of the parents. If teachers can develop an empathic understanding of the parent's position then it is much more likely that a productive parent–professional partnership will evolve.

Another important attitude which teachers need to have is hopeful but realistic views about the likely progress and eventual prognosis of the children with special needs with whom they work. Parents need teachers to be optimistic but objective about their children's development. They need teachers to be people of integrity who will not shy away from being open and honest with them but will do this with sensitivity. In addition, teachers need to communicate the attitude that nothing is hopeless and that every situation can be improved, even if perhaps not all of the problems experienced by parents can be completely solved.

KNOWLEDGE NEEDED TO WORK EFFECTIVELY WITH PARENTS

If teachers do exhibit some negative attitudes towards parents instead of the positive attitudes discussed above, then it is hardly surprising since the majority of them would have received little or no input on working with parents on their initial training courses or as a part of any subsequent in-service training. Their attitudes towards parents would therefore have been influenced by those of senior colleagues, by community attitudes to children with special needs and by their own ignorance of the reality of parenting such children.

Fortunately, in the last ten years or so, there has been a substantial growth in the number of publications on parents and there is now a large number of books and articles on the topic which provide information for professionals such as teachers (see References at the end of the book). The aim of this book is to highlight the essential knowledge required by teachers to work effectively with parents. In particular, it is considered essential that teachers have a good understanding of the processes and reactions which parents may experience in coming to terms with their child's special needs. It is also important that teachers are aware of the possible effects of the child on the family as a whole and on individual members of the family, such as mothers, fathers, siblings and grandparents. In addition, teachers need to know specifically what they can do to help parents of children with various types of special needs. These aspects are discussed in Chapters 3 and 4.

Teachers also need to have adequate knowledge of the special needs they are likely to encounter. There are already many excellent sources of such information (e.g. Batshaw *et al.*, 1992; Hallahan and Kauffman, 1991; Lansdown, 1980; Morgan, 1985). Teachers need to be knowledgeable about the range of services which are available to parents as well as sources of additional finance (Furneaux, 1988; Philip and Duckworth, 1982; Stone and Taylor, 1977). They also need to be familiar with all other possible sources of help for families of children with special needs, such as the parent support groups operating in the community where the family lives. Teachers need to know about typical attitudes towards children with special needs which exist in the community (McConkey and McCormack, 1983) and need to be aware of strategies for helping parents cope with prejudice and abuse (Fullwood and Cronin, 1986). Finally, teachers should be knowledgeable about the different reactions to disability, illness, divorce and death typical of various ethnic and cultural groups. They need to be sufficiently aware of the beliefs and customs of the ethnic groups with which they work to be able to adapt their interventions so that they are culturally appropriate (see Collins *et al.*, 1993).

SKILLS NEEDED TO WORK EFFECTIVELY WITH PARENTS

In addition to communicating appropriate attitudes and possessing relevant knowledge, in order to work effectively with parents, teachers need good interpersonal skills. An essential part of this is the possession of basic listening and counselling skills (Seligman, 1979; Turnbull and Turnbull, 1986). Other interpersonal skills required by teachers include the assertion skills needed for working with parents and for collaborating with colleagues in the special education field. Listening, counselling and assertion skills are discussed in Chapter 5.

Teachers also need the organizational and communication skills necessary for maintaining contact with parents through meetings, home visits, letters and telephone calls. These forms of contact are discussed in Chapter 6. In addition, teachers need the skills required for involving parents in their children's educational programmes such as in home–school reading schemes or home–school behaviour programmes. These programmes are discussed in Chapter 7. Finally, ideally, teachers need group leadership skills so that they can organize various group experiences for parents, such as parent education programmes. These are discussed in Chapter 8.

PARENTAL RIGHTS IN EDUCATION

The benefits of involving parents in their children's education first gained widespread acknowledgement from teachers in the 1960s following publication of the Plowden Report (DES, 1967) and reports on the projects conducted in educational priority areas, most of which involved working closely with parents. Legislation enacted in the last fifteen years has had the effect of increasing the importance of parental involvement in education since parents' rights have been substantially extended (Statham *et al.*, 1989; Wolfendale, 1992). The additional rights given to parents during this time are summarized below.

1980 Education Act

In this legislation parents were granted the right to choose the school they want to send their children to. Parents were also given the right to be represented on the governing bodies of schools. In addition, school governors and Local Education Authorities (LEAs) were required to provide written information to parents on such things as: admission criteria; the curriculum; examination results; discipline; and school organization.

1981 Education Act

This was the Act in which many of the recommendations of the Warnock Report (DES, 1978) were embodied. It was solely concerned with children with special needs. The Act gave parents the right to request the LEA to conduct a formal assessment of their children's special educational needs. It requires parent involvement in the assessment process and in annual reviews of their children's progress. It also gives parents the right to appeal against LEA decisions about their children. Further, it made it clear that parents' wishes should be taken into account when deciding whether or not to integrate children with special needs into ordinary schools.

1986 Education Act

The first of two Acts passed in 1986 required increased parental representation on the governing bodies of schools. Governors were required to present an annual report to parents and to have a meeting with parents at the school in order to discuss the report.

1988 Education Reform Act

This Act granted parents the right to send their children to any school of their choice so long as it has room for them. It also required that parents are sent an annual report on their children's progress. In addition it gave schools the opportunity of opting out of LEA control if a majority of parents voted in favour of this.

1992 Education Act

This Act set out new procedures for the inspection of schools, in which parents have an increased role. Parents have the right to meet with inspectors before the inspection to discuss any issues they wish. School staff and governors are not allowed to be present unless their children attend the school. Also, all parents are sent a questionnaire by the inspectors asking for their comments on the school. In addition, inspectors are expected to have discussions with parents on a wide range of issues concerning schools including the way schools involve parents in the identification and assessment of special educational needs and annual reviews of statements (Stone, 1993). Finally, parents have the right to receive a summary report on the results of the school inspection.

1993 Education Act

The Code of Practice which provides guidance on the implementation of the 1993 Act emphasizes the importance for schools of establishing partnerships with parents. It requires that schools should have written policy and procedures for:

- acting on parental concerns
- involving parents when teachers express concerns about their child
- incorporating parents' views in assessments and reviews of progress.

It also requires that schools provide parents with information on:

- the schools' policy for special educational needs (SEN)
- the support available for children with SEN within the school and LEA
- the services provided by local authorities for children with SEN
- parents' rights to be involved in assessment and decision-making
- voluntary organizations which can provide guidance or support.

In addition, it requires that schools ensure that parents have access to this information by providing:

- information in the community languages spoken by parents for whom English is not their first language
- information on tape for parents who have literacy difficulties
- a parents' room or other arrangements to help parents feel comfortable about coming to the school.

The effect of the 1993 Education Act will therefore be to further strengthen parental influence over the education of their children.

The increasing emphasis on parents' rights which has evolved through the above Education Acts means that schools can no longer afford *not* to work closely with parents. Of course, most schools already involve parents, including those who have children with special needs, in a variety of ways. Typical roles which parents fulfil in schools are discussed below.

PARENTAL ROLES IN EDUCATION

Eight ways in which schools typically involve parents have been described by Morgan (1993) as: recipients of information; governors; helpers; fund-raisers; experts; clients; co-educators; and consultants. These parental roles are discussed below.

Recipients of information

Parents have traditionally been on the receiving end of information from schools. There has been information about the school, such as what it offers to pupils and what it requires from pupils and their parents. There has also been information about the progress and behaviour of the pupils which has been conveyed to parents by means of annual reports and parent–teacher meetings. Following the 1992 and 1993 Education Acts there is to be a marked increase in the amount of information conveyed to parents. For example, at the completion of school inspections parents are to be sent a report summarizing the findings of the inspection team. Another example is that parents are to receive an annual report from governors on the school's policy and provisions for pupils with special educational needs. Therefore, an important role of parents is to be able to deal appropriately with the increasing amount of information they receive from schools.

Governors

As noted above, the role of parents as school governors has increased substantially in recent years. The 1980 Education Act required that the governing bodies of schools must include two parents. The 1986 Act extended this by prescribing that the number of parent governors should vary according to the size of the school, such that small schools would have two parents and large schools would have five parents. The 1988, 1992 and 1993 Acts have increased the duties of school governors and it is now stipulated that one governor takes specific responsibility for oversight of the school's policy and practice concerning children with special educational needs.

Therefore, recent years have seen a significant increase in the number of parents acting as school governors and a parallel increase in their influence on what goes on in schools. Unfortunately, these changes have generally not been accompanied by opportunities for parent governors to receive the training necessary for them to competently fulfil their roles (Scott, 1993). This is particularly important for the governor who has the responsibility for special educational needs, who should have up-to-date knowledge of appropriate ways of identifying and providing for children with such needs within the school.

Helpers

Many parents are involved in schools as voluntary helpers. Parents fulfil a wide range of helping roles, including such activities as: preparing classroom materials; listening to children read; and accompanying classes on a school visit. Parents also help by sharing particular skills which they have developed such as craft activities or specialist knowledge of a particular subject.

The use of parent helpers varies widely from school to school. I have visited some mainstream and some special schools in which highly effective volunteer programmes have been running. However, in many schools parent helpers remain a largely untapped resource. This is probably because some teachers are put off such schemes by the fact that a small minority of parents who offer to help will create difficulties, perhaps by overstepping their role or by upsetting pupils or other parents. However, this is a reason for being careful in setting up and monitoring parent helper schemes, not for avoiding this aspect of parent involvement altogether. This potential difficulty perhaps explains why the best programmes I have seen have been tightly organized with the helping tasks carefully specified and the programmes closely monitored by teachers.

Fund-raisers

Raising money for the school, by such means as cake stalls and fun runs, has long been an important role which parents have played in the schools which their children have attended. It is probably of even greater importance in these times when less money is forthcoming from the Government and schools are expected to raise funds for items, such as computers, which many people regard as essential equipment in today's world.

In the past, fund-raising was viewed by some teachers as the most important or perhaps even the only role which parents should play in schools. The main aim of parent–teacher associations was often considered to be fund-raising. This is not so much the case in the 1990s when parents are being expected to fulfil various roles in schools, as is documented in this section.

Experts

A key contribution which most parents make to the functioning of schools is by providing teachers with valuable information about their children. This is particularly important for parents who have children with special needs. Parents need to pass on to teachers information about their children's disabilities, about any medication which they take and about family circumstances. Parents also need to inform teachers about such things as the likely effects of a family bereavement or a medical condition on the child's behaviour.

It is only recently that parents are beginning to be considered to be the experts on their children. In the past, professionals have tended to undervalue the knowledge which parents have of their children. This has resulted in many parents feeling frustrated that professionals such as teachers have tended to talk *at* them rather than listen to what they have to say. This situation is changing and it is now realized by many teachers that while they are the experts on education, parents are the experts on their children.

Co-educators

Many parents are now involved in projects which cast them in the role of co-educators, along with teachers, of their children. The involvement of parents ranges from such activities as checking homework diaries, through listening to children read, to highly structured schemes like the Portage programme (Topping, 1986). Home–school programmes have been reported in a wide range of curriculum areas such as reading, maths, science and European awareness, in addition to programmes which focus on children's behaviour. Acting as a co-educator is a key role for parents and is one which more and more of them are wanting to play. The involvement of parents as co-educators is discussed in Chapter 7.

Clients

Since the advent of open enrolment and Local Management of Schools parents' roles as clients or consumers have come to the fore. Parents now have a much bigger say in deciding which school their children will attend. For parents of children with special educational needs this role has been reinforced by the 1993 Education Act. This requires that schools chosen for children with SEN should be in accordance with parents' wishes and, further, that a school named in a child's statement of SEN must accept that child into the school.

These changes have meant that schools now view parents as potential customers whom they must attract to the school and for whom they may need to compete with other schools. Now that schools have a vested interest in attracting parents and keeping them satisfied, greater importance is attached to the need for all teachers to develop effective working relationships with parents.

Consultants

One consequence of the 1992 Education Act is that parents are being cast in the role of consultants to schools. As stated earlier, this Act requires that, before a school inspection begins, parents are to be consulted about how well the school functions both by a questionnaire sent to their homes and by the opportunity to attend a meeting with the inspectors. Areas of concern can then be investigated by the inspection team. This represents a major change from the past when parents tended to be consulted about peripheral issues, such as school uniforms, but not about central aspects of the school, such as the curriculum and the maintainance of discipline. Schools will therefore need to become much more aware of how they are viewed by parents, of what parents see as strengths and weaknesses in the school's organization and be prepared to respond to these.

SUMMARY AND CONCLUSIONS

This book is aimed at helping teachers develop effective working relationships with parents. The first chapter has provided a rationale for this enterprise and outlined the attitudes, skills and knowledge which teachers need to develop. It is considered that, because of the widely varying roles which parents can play in schools and the increases in parental rights, both of which have been discussed in this chapter, it has become essential for schools to develop an appropriate philosophy or policy for working with parents (see Wolfendale, 1992). Such a policy needs to be clear about parents' rights to participate in various aspects of school life. It needs to embody the idea of a working relationship based on equality of value of contributions from parents and teachers. This involves acknowledging the different responsibilities but shared accountability of both parents and teachers within a working alliance formed on behalf of children. It also needs to embody the concept of equal opportunities for involvement of parents from a wide range of cultural backgrounds. This involves ensuring that all necessary means are used to overcome language barriers and that teachers avoid being judgemental when they encounter parents with different values and attitudes to child rearing.

In the following chapter, various approaches to working with parents are discussed and a model is presented which is designed to facilitate implementation of the school's policy on parental involvement and to provide a guide to professional practice with parents.

—2—
Model for parent involvement

INTRODUCTION

A few years ago I was invited to India to lead workshops on counselling skills for professionals working with mentally handicapped children and their parents. The participants in most of the workshops were teachers but on one particular day in Bangalore I was asked to work with a group which included approximately 30 teachers and 20 parents. Because it was such a large mixed group I decided to use an idea which I had learned from a colleague, Milton Seligman of the University of Pittsburgh, who had led a workshop with parents and professionals in New Zealand several years earlier.

I divided the participants into five groups with about ten members each. Teachers and parents were in separate groups. I then announced the tasks, which for the parent groups was to discuss and report back on 'What we want from teachers' and for the teacher groups was to discuss and report back on 'What we want from parents'. When the groups reported back on their lists I was struck by how similar they were to the lists produced by the parents and teachers in the New Zealand workshop.

The main things that parents wanted from teachers were:

- teachers to consult them more and listen to their points of view
- a say in planning their children's educational programmes
- teachers to be aware of their family circumstances when suggesting tasks which could be done at home
- a more open attitude from teachers, for example, a willingness to admit it when they didn't know something
- teachers to concentrate less on academic tasks such as reading and more on skills for daily living such as communication and self-help skills
- regular interaction, including home visits by teachers.

The main things teachers wanted from parents were:

- parents to co-operate in reinforcing school programmes at home
- both parents, if possible, to come into school more often

- parents to encourage their children to be as independent as possible rather than to overprotect them
- parents to have realistic expectations of what their children were capable of doing
- parents to be open with them about any circumstances at home which could affect their children's performance at school.

The value of this exercise to the participants is that it clarifies expectations on both sides. In both the Indian and New Zealand workshops there was genuine surprise on the part of many teachers and parents regarding some of the expectations placed on them. This suggests that there is insufficient consideration given to the conduct of relationships between professionals and parents. It seems that assumptions are often made on both sides without these being made explicit. This raises the issue of the appropriateness of various approaches to parent–professional relationships.

APPROACHES TO PARENT–PROFESSIONAL RELATIONSHIPS

Cunningham and Davis (1985) have proposed that there are three general approaches to parent–professional relationships which are currently in use in the field of education. These are the expert, transplant and consumer models. The three models will now be discussed and the concept of partnership between professionals and parents considered.

Expert model

In this model professionals regard themselves as the experts on all aspects of the functioning of children with special needs and parents' views are accorded little credence. Professionals maintain control over decisions while the parents' role is to receive information and instructions from professionals about their children with special needs. A major problem with this approach is that it encourages parents to be submissive and dependent on professionals. Parents are reluctant to question professional decisions and tend to lose faith in their own competence. Another problem is that, because professionals do not make use of the rich source of knowledge parents have about their children, they tend to overlook important problems or abilities which the children have. In addition, professionals working within the expert model will not be aware of any difficulties the parents themselves might experience. All these factors increase the possibility that parents will be dissatisfied with the service they get from professionals who adopt this approach.

A startling example of a professional operating within the framework of the expert model is provided by Roos (1978) who reports on attempts he and his wife made to obtain a diagnosis of their daughter's disability:

> Our pediatrician next referred us to a neurologist. Since this worthy professional was a consultant to the large state institution for the retarded of which I was the superintendant, I felt confident that he would immediately recognize the obvious signs of severe retardation in our child. Imagine my consternation when . . . the learned consultant cast a baleful eye on my wife and me and informed us that the child was quite normal. On the other hand, he continued, her parents were obviously neurotically anxious and he would prescribe tranquilizers for us. (p. 246)

What is particularly remarkable about this professional was that his adherence to the expert model was so strong that even when faced with senior colleagues working in the disability field, who were placed in the role of parents, he still had no doubt that he was right and the parents were wrong.

Transplant model

This model is employed by professionals who regard themselves as the main sources of expertise on children with special needs but who recognize the benefits of using parents as a resource. They consider that some of their expertise can be transplanted from them into parents so that parents can carry out some form of intervention with their children. A well-known example of this approach in the field of education is a paired reading programme in which parents are trained to help their children with reading at home (Topping, 1986).

In this model the professional remains in control and decides on the interventions to be used but does accept that parents can play an important part in facilitating their children's progress. Therefore, there is more likelihood that parents' views will be considered and their concerns addressed. However, in order to use this approach professionals do need additional skills such as techniques for effectively training parents and the interpersonal skills required for establishing a productive working relationship with parents. These factors will increase the likelihood of parents' being satisfied with the service they receive and reduce the tendency for them to become dependent on professionals.

The danger of this approach for the professionals who use it is to assume that all parents can and should take on the role of acting as a resource, thereby risking overburdening some parents by placing excessive demands on them to carry out intervention programmes with their children. The chances of this happening are increased for children whose special needs are complex or severe since several different professionals, such as speech therapists, psychologists and teachers, may all be expecting parents to carry out intervention programmes in the home.

Consumer model

In this model parents are regarded as being consumers of professional services. The professional acts as a consultant while the parent decides what action is to be taken. The parent has control over the decision-making process while professionals provide them with relevant information and a range of options from which to choose. Thus, in this approach, the professional defers to parents, who are effectively placed in the expert role. The professional's role is to listen to parents' views and help them choose from the alternatives available. Because parents are in control of the decision-making process in this approach they are likely to be much more satisfied with the service they receive, to feel more competent about their parenting, and are also less likely to become dependent on professionals.

The danger of this approach is that, taken to its extreme, it can lead to an abdication of professional responsibility. I have seen this occur, while working as an educational psychologist, when a colleague adopted an extreme form of the consumer model. This psychologist would handle the selection of an appropriate educational placement for a child with special needs by simply showing parents around a variety of schools and classes and getting them to choose one. Without the benefit of relevant information and guidance about the likely advantages and disadvantages of each potential placement for the child in question, from the professional supposedly knowledgeable about how special needs can be most effectively met, parents were encouraged to make uninformed decisions which may not have been in their children's best interests. In this way parents were placed in the role of experts on how their children's special needs could be met. This seems to me to be just as inappropriate as professionals regarding themselves as experts on all aspects of children's functioning, and therefore adopting the expert model in their relationships with parents.

Partnership

I consider that the most appropriate model for relationships between teachers and parents is one in which teachers are viewed as being experts on education and parents are viewed as being experts on their children. The relationship between teachers and parents can then be a partnership which involves the sharing of expertise and control in order to provide the optimum education for children with special needs (Mittler and McConachie, 1983). Parents and teachers contribute different strengths to their relationship, thereby increasing the potency of the partnership. For example, most parents have strong emotional attachments to their children and therefore make excellent advocates for them. However, the emotional attachment also tends to make them somewhat subjective when considering their children's abilities and needs, which is why the objectivity that teachers bring to the partnership is so important (Cunningham and Davis, 1985).

The *Code of Practice on the Identification and Assessment of Special Educational Needs* emphasizes the importance of establishing a partnership with parents. It suggests that this partnership '. . . has a crucial bearing on the child's educational progress and the effectiveness of any school-based action' (p. 12). It goes on to say:

> Children's progress will be diminished if their parents are not seen as partners in the educational process with unique knowledge to impart. Professional help can seldom be effective unless it builds on parents' capacity to be involved and unless parents consider that professionals take account of what they say and treat their views and anxieties as intrinsically important. (p. 13)

Therefore, an essential aspect of the partnership is that it must be based on mutual respect. For example, it requires parents and teachers to listen to each other and give due consideration to each other's views. In this way an effective collaborative working relationship can be established.

However, having the partnership model as an overall guide does not preclude the use of interventions based on the other approaches when they would be more appropriate. For example, the transplant model quite correctly provides the underlying rationale of many of the parent involvement projects, such as home–school reading schemes, described in Chapter 7. Also, the adoption of the expert model is justified in prescribing treatment, such as personal therapy or parenting skills programmes, for parents who have subjected their children to physical, emotional or sexual abuse (see Morgan, 1985; Walker *et al.*, 1988).

In fact, some interventions, such as the parent education programmes described in Chapter 8, can be organized from different perspectives depending on the group of parents to be involved. That is, they can be organized from the perspective of the consumer model with parents stipulating what guidance or input they would like. Alternatively, they can be organized from the perspective of the expert model with professionals specifying what parents need to learn. For example, parents of children with disabilities may be able and willing to select suitable input (consumer model) whereas parents who have subjected their children to some form of abuse are likely to need professionals to decide what input would be most beneficial (expert).

Therefore, although there must be enough flexibility to enable other models to be used when necessary, it is considered that the partnership model is generally the most appropriate perspective from which to develop a constructive working relationship with parents. In this relationship, teachers should be aware of addressing parents' needs and of acknowledging the various ways they can contribute to the development and education of their children with special needs. This will facilitate the development of effective partnerships between parents and teachers. In order for such partnerships to become more than just lofty ideals the concept needs to be developed into a formal model for parent involvement designed to guide practice. This is considered in the next section.

THE NEED FOR A MODEL OF PARENT INVOLVEMENT

The evolution of parent involvement in Britain has, so far, tended to be practice-led rather than being guided by theory or policy (Atkin *et al.*, 1988). Many examples of interesting parent involvement projects are in existence around the country and useful models are available for various types of parent involvement. Also, numerous books have been published in the last few years on the topic of parent involvement with parents in general (e.g. Bastiani, 1987, 1988, 1989; Cyster *et al.*, 1979; Griffiths and Hamilton, 1984; Harding and Pike, 1988; Jowett *et al.*, 1991; Lombana, 1983; Pugh and De'Ath, 1984; Sullivan, 1988; Tizard *et al.*, 1981; Topping, 1986; Wolfendale, 1983, 1992). There have also been a plethora of books on the topic of working with parents of children with disabilities (e.g. Cunningham and Davis, 1985; Gargiulo, 1985; Kroth, 1985; McConkey, 1985; Seligman, 1979; Simpson, 1990; Stewart, 1986). These have been written with the intention of providing teachers and other professionals with the knowledge necessary to build effective relationships with parents.

In addition, several theoretical models are now available which are designed to provide teachers with frameworks with which to formulate overall policy and plans for working with parents. Such models enable each school to conduct an audit of their current practice with regard to parent involvement in order to ensure that, as far as possible, parents' needs are being met and their potential contributions are being utilized.

MODEL FOR PARENT INVOLVEMENT

The theoretical model for parent involvement described below was developed by combining and adapting existing models (e.g. Bastiani, 1989; Kroth, 1985; Lombana, 1983; Wolfendale, 1992) and by gaining feedback from numerous groups of parents and teachers. The model was originally devised with teachers of children with special needs in mind (Hornby, 1989) but it was subsequently realized that, with slight adaptations, it was equally applicable to all teachers, including those working in mainstream schools and those in special schools (Hornby, 1990). The model for parent involvement is presented in Figure 2.1.

The model consists of two pyramids, one representing a hierarchy of parents' needs, the other a hierarchy of parents' strengths or possible contributions. Both pyramids demonstrate visually the different levels of needs and contributions of parents. Thus, while all parents have some needs and some potential contributions which can be utilized, a smaller number have an intense need for guidance, or the capability of making an extensive contribution. The model also shows that, for parents' needs at a higher level, more time and expertise is required by teachers in order to meet these needs. Similarly, the parents who make a greater contribution require a higher level of expertise and time available.

Each of the components of the model will now be outlined and the knowledge and skills needed by teachers in order to participate in each type of parent involvement will be identified.

Contributions by parents

Information All parents can contribute valuable information about their children with special needs because they have known them throughout their lives and have been the ones who have participated in all previous contacts with professionals in order to assess and plan for meeting their children's needs. Information concerning children's likes and dislikes, strengths and weaknesses, along with any relevant medical details can be gathered by teachers at parent–teacher meetings. Many parents feel more comfortable on their own territory and generally appreciate it when teachers offer to visit them. This also provides an opportunity to observe how parents cope with their children with special needs at home and to

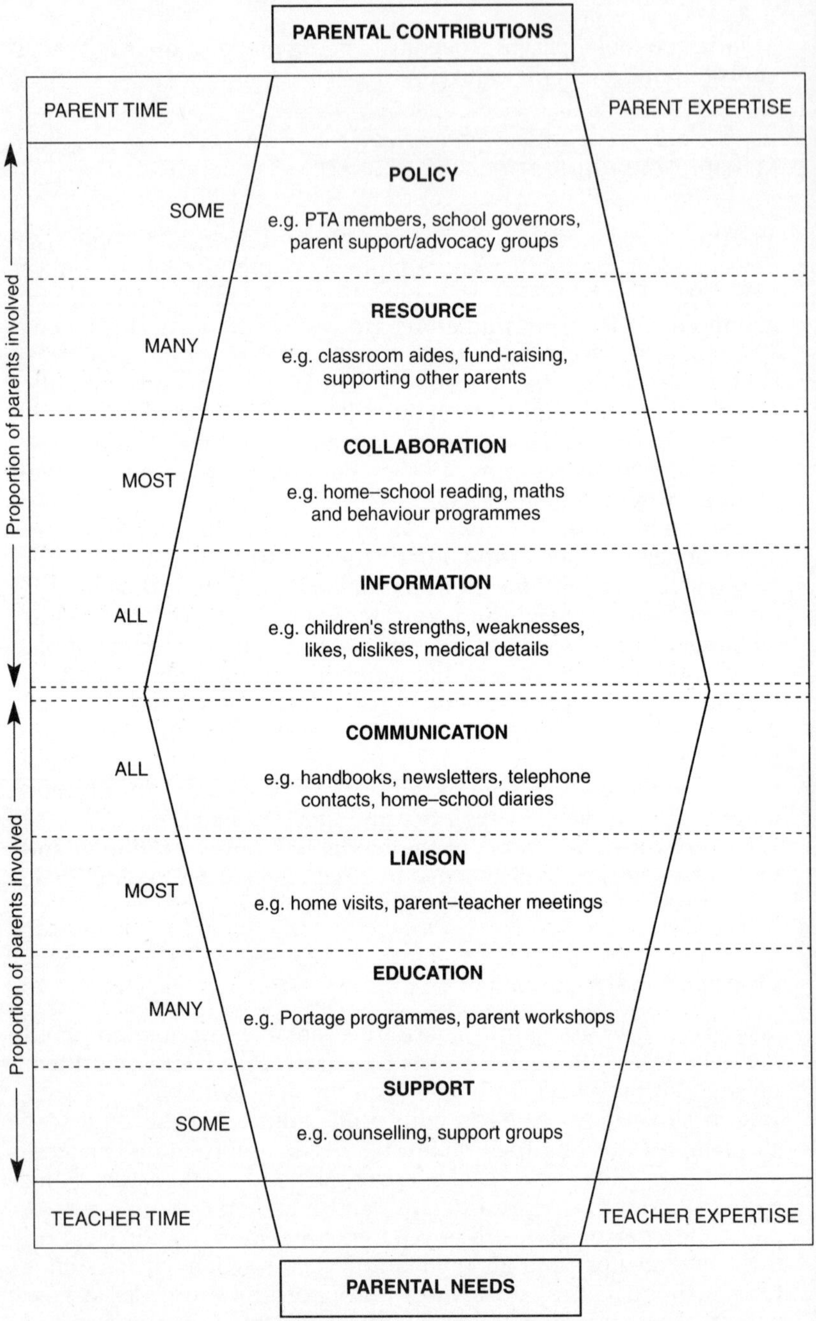

Figure 2.1 *Model for parent involvement*

learn about any relevant family circumstances. Making full use of parents' knowledge of their children not only leads to more effective professional practice, it also makes parents feel that they have been listened to and that an active interest has been taken in their children. Therefore, teachers need to develop good listening and interviewing skills (Atkin *et al.*, 1988; Seligman, 1979). In addition, they need to be knowledgeable about how family dynamics are affected by children with special needs and to be aware of the possible effects on other family members (see Chapter 3).

Collaboration Most parents are willing and able to contribute more than just information. Most parents are able to collaborate with teachers by reinforcing classroom programmes at home, such as in home–school reading programmes (Griffiths and Hamilton, 1984; Topping, 1986). However, some parents, at some times, are not willing to carry out work at home with their children. This can be very frustrating for teachers since they realize that collaboration between home and school generally results in children making greater progress, so that children whose parents do not work closely with them are likely to develop more slowly. However, I have come to believe that teachers have to accept that some parents at some points in time are simply not able to collaborate in this way. It is probably because their resources are already fully committed in coping with their children at home, so they are not able to do anything extra. At a later time family circumstances may change and parents may then want to become more involved in their children's education. Professionals must respect parents' rights to make this decision in consideration of the wider needs of their families. So, while involvement in home–school programmes, or other requests for parents to carry out work with their children at home, should always be offered to all parents, including those who have not collaborated in the past, it should be expected that a small proportion of parents will not participate. Therefore, teachers need the skills of collaborating with parents in a flexible partnership in which parents' choices are respected.

Resource Many parents have the time and ability to act as voluntary teacher aides, assisting either in the classroom, or in the preparation of materials, or in fund-raising. Others may have special skills which they can contribute such as helping prepare newsletters, in craft activities, or in curriculum areas in which they have a special talent. Some parents may have the time, skills and knowledge to provide support to other parents either informally or perhaps through participation in self-help or support groups such as Parent to Parent schemes (see Chapter 8).

In these times of contracting professional resources teachers should make sure that they make optimum use of this valuable voluntary resource. However, too often this doesn't happen, as is illustrated by an incident which occurred when I was presenting the parent involvement model to a group of parents and teachers at a special school. When I came to the part on parents acting as a resource, the headteacher commented that parents were encouraged to come into the school to help in this way. Immediately, a parent responded that her child had been in the school for three years and she didn't know about this. This incident highlights the fact that invitations for parents to help at the school need to be repeated at least annually by such means as newsletters.

It is often the case that parents also benefit from acting as a resource. They may acquire knowledge which is helpful to their understanding of their own children. In addition, they are often observed to gain in confidence through helping others rather than always being the ones to receive help. In order to enable as many parents as possible to act as a resource to the school teachers need practical management and communication skills (Kroth, 1985).

Policy Some parents are able to contribute their expertise through membership of parent or professional organizations. This includes being a school governor, a lay inspector, a member of the parent–teacher association (PTA), or being involved in a parent support or advocacy group. Others have the time and ability to provide in-service training for professionals by speaking at conferences or workshops, or by writing about their experiences (e.g. Featherstone, 1981). Teachers should continually be on the lookout for parents who can contribute in this way so that their abilities can be used to the full (Sullivan, 1988).

Parents can influence school policy on children with special needs through their involvement as a governor or PTA member. They can also sometimes influence government policy on children with special educational needs through their involvement in groups such as MENCAP and Scope (formerly the Spastics Society). One of the most exciting things about the development of Parent to Parent schemes (discussed in Chapter 8) in New Zealand was that, because they involve parents of children with a wide range of disabilities, links were formed between parents who were active in groups concerned with children with learning difficulties, hearing impairment, visual impairment and physical disability. Through these links an alliance of parents representing several disability groups was formed. Because of this broad representation the alliance had more impact on the government than had previously come from the individual organizations and therefore initiated significant changes in the legislation regarding children with special needs.

Needs of parents

Communication All parents need to have effective channels of communication with all the professionals who work with their children, especially their teachers. They need information about the organization and requirements of the school as it affects their child. They need to know when their children are to be assessed and when a change of placement is being considered. That is, all parents need to know about their rights and responsibilities. This can be provided through handbooks or regular newsletters written especially for parents.

Parents need to feel that they can contact the school at any time when they have a concern about their child. Some parents prefer to communicate by telephone, others would rather call in to see the teacher face to face, while still others find that contact through written notes or home–school diaries suits them best. Therefore, educators need to develop effective written and oral communication skills and ensure that a wide range of communication options are open to parents. However, the most important factor in maintaining good communication is the openness to parents which schools demonstrate through their contacts with parents. The attitude of choice has often been referred to as an 'open-door policy' in which parents feel comfortable about contacting, or going into, the school when they have a concern (Bastiani, 1987; Harding and Pike, 1988).

Liaison Most parents want to know how their children are getting on at school. They want to find out what their children have achieved and whether they are having any difficulties. They regard teachers as the main source of information on their children's performance at school and therefore need to have a working partnership with them. Teachers can facilitate this by keeping in regular contact with parents through such means as telephone calls, home visits, home–school notebooks, weekly report cards and by meeting with parents at school. These strategies are discussed in detail in Chapter 6.

Teachers of children with special needs are often disappointed that some parents do not come to parent–teacher meetings at school, thereby giving the impression that they are not interested in how their children are getting on. In my experience, there are usually other reasons for them not turning up, such as the difficulties involved in getting a babysitter, the overwhelming demands of looking after their family, or anxieties about coming to school related to the negative experiences they had at school. It is important, then, for teachers to find other ways of liaising with these parents, perhaps by having regular telephone contacts or home visits.

Therefore, teachers need to develop the skills of conducting formal and informal meetings with parents. In addition, they need to offer a range of options for liaison with parents so that those who do not feel comfortable coming to formal meetings have other forms of regular contact made available to them (Cyster *et al.*, 1979; Howard and Hollingsworth, 1985; Simpson, 1990).

Education Many parents are interested in participating in parent education (or parent training) programmes aimed at promoting their children's progress or managing their behaviour. Parent education can be conducted individually, as in the Portage programme (White and Cameron, 1988), or in parent groups or workshops, which are widely reported in the literature (McConkey, 1985; Topping, 1986). Some parents will not want to take part in such programmes, for a variety of reasons. There will be those who, at a certain point in time, feel confident about the way they are parenting their children with special needs and don't see the need for parent education. Later, when their children reach a different developmental stage they may think differently. For other parents, there will be practical difficulties such as arranging babysitters or transport. However, in my experience, a substantial number of parents are interested in being involved in parent training and most of those who do participate get a tremendous amount out of it. Ideally then, opportunities for taking part in either individual or group parent education should be made available to all parents.

It seems that the most effective format for parent education is one which combines guidance about promoting children's development with opportunities for parents to discuss their concerns (Pugh and De'Ath, 1984). For example, teachers who use the Portage programme with parents of young children with special needs find that they are most effective when they spend about half their time listening to and talking with the parents (White and Cameron, 1988). Professionals involved in parent education therefore need listening and counselling skills in addition to their teaching skills. The interpersonal skills needed by teachers in their work with parents are discussed in Chapter 5.

Parent education programmes which involve a group of parents, and employ a workshop format, easily lend themselves to providing a combination of educational input and sharing of concerns. This type of format enables parents to learn new skills and gain confidence through talking to other parents and professionals (Hornby and Murray, 1983). In order to conduct such workshops teachers need to develop organizational skills and the skills of group facilitation. Group work with parents is discussed in Chapter 8.

Support Some parents, at some times, are in need of supportive counselling, even though they may not actually request it. This support can be provided either individually or in group counselling programmes, or workshops, as noted above. Although such support should be available to all parents, from diagnosis of the disability onwards, the majority of parents seldom need extensive counselling. In the past it has often been assumed that the greatest need of parents of children with special needs is counselling in order to help them come to terms with their child's disability. This has led to an overemphasis on this aspect of parent involvement to the detriment of the other aspects, such as communication and liaison, which have been discussed above. The fact is, that if parents have good channels of communication and regular liaison with teachers, coupled with the opportunity to receive guidance about their children whenever they need it, then only a few of them will need counselling at any particular time.

Whereas most British parents are reluctant to seek the help of professional counsellors, they will approach their children's teachers in search of guidance or counselling for the problems which concern them. Teachers should therefore have a level of basic counselling skills sufficient to be good listeners and to help parents solve everyday problems. They should also have the knowledge necessary to be able to refer parents to professional counsellors when problems raised are beyond their level of competence. Alternatively, parents can be referred to parent support groups, such as Parent to Parent schemes in which parents have been professionally trained in counselling skills in order to provide supportive counselling to other parents. Parent to Parent schemes are described in Chapter 8 and counselling skills are discussed in Chapter 5.

USING THE MODEL TO GUIDE PARENT INVOLVEMENT PRACTICE

Using the model of parent involvement described here a comprehensive scheme of involvement can be designed to suit each school. The model can be used to generate a check-list designed to ensure that procedures are in place to meet parents' needs and to make sure that parents' potential contributions are being fully utilized. The check-list which follows has been adapted from a previous check-list on parent–professional relationships (Mittler, undated). It provides an example of the kinds of questions which teachers need to ask themselves when reviewing their school's policy and practice regarding parent involvement. Each level of the model for parent involvement will now be considered in turn and questions posed for teachers to consider.

Policy

- *Does the school have a separate written policy on parent involvement?* Does the policy clearly specify parents' rights and responsibilities and is it included in material distributed to all parents and teachers?
- *Have parents been involved in the formulation of this policy?* For example, have the PTA or parent governors had input into the policy design process?
- *What monitoring procedures are in place to ensure that the policy is implemented?* For example, how is feedback obtained from parents?
- *Is there an active Parent–Teacher Association (PTA) at the school?* What can be done to encourage more parents to participate in PTA activities?
- *What involvement do parents have in discussions about the aims of the school, the curriculum and other issues such as parent–teacher relationships?* For example, are parents' views sought about the school's policy for meeting special educational needs?
- *Is there a room set aside for parents' use?* Do parents use a spare classroom, or can the staffroom be used by parents during lesson times?
- *What means are there for encouraging parents to become school governors?* Are all teachers on the lookout for parents who would be effective in this role?
- *Are parents involved in in-service training?* For example, have parents of children with SEN been invited to talk about their experiences, expectations, needs and possible contributions?
- *Who is responsible for ensuring that parents with a particular talent for leadership are identified and encouraged to put their abilities to use?* Who identifies parents who could contribute in capacities within the school such as on the PTA or governing body, or outside the school in organizations such as MENCAP, CRUSE or Parent to Parent schemes?

Resource

- *In what kinds of activities does the school welcome help from parents?* Are parents used to listen to children read or to assist in teaching or in preparing classroom materials?
- *How are parents informed about the ways in which they can help at the school?* Is there a parents' handbook or a regular newsletter?
- *How is voluntary help from parents organized within the school?* For example, is a particular member of staff assigned to co-ordinate the help or is it seen as the responsibility of each teacher?

Collaboration

- *How do parents contribute to the assessment of their child's needs?* For example, by being asked for their observations or by completing developmental check-lists.
- *How are the results of school assessments communicated to parents?* Are individual parent–teacher meetings scheduled?
- *What input do parents have in deciding the goals and teaching priorities for their children?* For example, do parents discuss with teachers the emphasis which should be placed on developing basic academic skills or social skills, as opposed to following the National Curriculum?
- *How are parents involved in developing their child's Individual Educational Plan (IEP)?* For example, do they attend all the meetings and have a chance to discuss their child with any outside specialists involved, such as peripatetic teachers, educational psychologists or speech therapists?
- *How are parents encouraged to reinforce school programmes at home?* For example, are they expected to participate in a paired reading scheme or are they asked to work on developing daily living skills?
- *Are parents given a choice about the level of their involvement at home with their children?* Is there discussion with parents beforehand so that they are not pressured into projects which they cannot afford the time or energy to carry out?
- *How is parental involvement in reviews of their children's progress optimized?* For example, by obtaining their observations beforehand and being an active member of the review team.

Information

- *How is information on children with SEN, and on relevant family circumstances, gathered from parents?* Are home visits used in addition to parent–teacher meetings at school?

- *How is relevant information from parents disseminated to all members of staff who work with their children?* What systems are used to record, and communicate to teachers, information about such things as children's disabilities and the medication they require?
- *What use is made of parents' insights on their children?* For example, parents' knowledge of their children's strengths and weaknesses, likes and dislikes, or how they respond to different approaches.

Communication

- *What activities are used to ensure that all parents establish contact with the school?* Are performances or exhibitions of work by the pupils, social occasions or talks by well-known invited speakers used to attract large numbers of parents into the school?
- *How does the school pass on information to parents about their rights and responsibilities and about school organization?* For example, is this information disseminated by means of newsletters and hand-books specifically aimed at parents or by holding meetings at which school policies are discussed?
- *Does the school have balanced procedures for contacting parents?* That is, are parents contacted to inform them of their children's achievements as well as their difficulties or are they only contacted when there is a problem?
- *Does a member of staff visit families before pupils with SEN start to attend the school?* Are home visits scheduled when children are changing schools, moving from primary to secondary school, or being reintegrated following a period in a special school?
- *What guidelines are available for parents on visiting the school to talk over a concern with their children's teachers?* For example, do they have to go through the headteacher, make an appointment directly with the teacher, or just come in whenever they can?
- *What channels of communication are there between parents and teachers?* That is, can parents choose to telephone, write notes or frequently call in to the school?

Liaison

- *What are the frequency and purpose of parent–teacher meetings?* For example, are parents invited to attend termly meetings to review their children's IEPs or annual meetings to review statements?
- *Do parents regularly receive home visits?* Are home visits made at least once a year, or only when there is a problem? Are visits made by class teachers or senior members of staff? Is there flexibility in the time of day used so that both parents can be present?

- *How are home–school diaries used?* For example, are they used for all children or just for ones with SEN or for those with behavioural difficulties? Are diaries used daily or weekly?
- *What kinds of formal reports are sent home?* Are reports sent termly or yearly? Are progress reports sent separately to records of achievement?

Education

- *Are parents invited into the school to observe teaching in progress?* For example, are they invited to observe either their own child or other children in the school?
- *When are teachers available to provide guidance to parents?* Do teachers make home visits in order to provide guidance to parents or does this only occur in parent–teacher meetings at school?
- *Are parent workshops organized by the school?* For example, are there workshops for parents of children with reading difficulties or behaviour problems or for parents whose children are about to leave school?
- *Are parents informed about opportunities for parent education in the community?* Is information about parenting courses provided by Adult Education Centres or universities made available to parents?

Support

- *How are parents given opportunities to discuss their concerns on a one-to-one basis?* For example, is this done on home visits or in specially scheduled parent–teacher meetings at school?
- *Are opportunities provided for parents to share their concerns with other parents?* For example, are parents introduced to other parents who have children with similar difficulties? Are they given the opportunity of attending group counselling programmes or parent workshops?
- *Do teachers know where to refer parents for supportive counselling?* Is there an awareness of services and groups within the local community which can provide supportive counselling such as social workers, self-help groups or Parent to Parent schemes?
- *Are parents encouraged to participate in support groups and parent organizations outside the school?* For example, MENCAP, CRUSE and Parent to Parent schemes.

SUMMARY AND CONCLUSIONS

The expectations of parents and teachers of each other which emerged from workshops in different parts of the world were presented in order to suggest that, in the past, insufficient attention has been paid to parent–teacher relationships. Professional approaches to working with parents based on expert, transplant, consumer and partnership models were used to clarify the form of parent–teacher relationship which is considered to be the most productive. It was suggested that a theoretical model for parent involvement is needed in order to assist schools to design policies and procedures for involving parents. The model proposed addresses parents' needs and their potential contributions and suggests competencies needed by teachers in order to ensure its successful implementation. The model is then used to generate a check-list of questions which schools can use to evaluate their practice of parent involvement and identify strengths and areas which need further development.

However, for schemes of parent involvement to be successful, teachers must develop the knowledge and skills referred to in this chapter. Thus, it is important that pre-service and in-service training in the relevant knowledge, and counselling and communication skills, is provided for all teachers. In order to facilitate this process the following two chapters will address the knowledge required by teachers of children with special needs of various kinds. These will be followed by two chapters which will discuss the counselling and communication skills needed by teachers.

Understanding parents' reactions and needs

INTRODUCTION

One of the most harrowing and yet moving experiences I have ever had occurred when I was invited to speak to a support group for parents who had had a child who died. My brief was to talk about the reactions parents go through in coping with this loss and to facilitate parental sharing of their own experiences and feelings with each other. I decided to use the model of adaptation to loss, which is described below, as a catalyst to promote discussion. I had got about halfway through describing the stages of reaction when the first parent burst into tears and left the room! While the social worker who had invited me to speak comforted this parent I nervously continued presenting the model.

When I had finished describing the model, mothers and fathers talked freely about the losses they were trying to cope with. Parents who had lost children and young adults through car accidents, cancer and suicide expressed intense feelings and some of them shed tears. My overall reaction was one of helplessness in the face of the intense need for help which these parents clearly had. Having your child die is said to be the most difficult bereavement to cope with, since it goes against the normal order of events in life (Worden, 1991). After attending the meeting I can certainly agree with that.

I had developed the model for adaptation to loss through work with parents of children with various disabilities. Many parents have told me that the model has been useful in helping them explain the process which they experienced in coming to terms with their child's disability. It has also been used with parents of children with serious illnesses, such as heart problems, where it has been found useful in helping parents to open up and talk about their experiences and feelings.

In this chapter, the model of adaptation to loss will be described along with other perspectives on the process which parents typically experience in coming to terms with the discovery that their child has a serious illness, a disability or a psychological problem. The various perspectives on the process of parental adaptation are provided in order to alert teachers to the wide range of reactions which parents may experience. Of course, how parents react to and cope with the discovery that their child has special needs will differ from parent to parent. The various models and perspectives are presented in order to describe possible parental reactions, not to suggest that all parents will necessarily experience some or any of them. Later in the chapter, consideration will be given to how children with disabilities or other difficulties typically affect and are affected by the functioning of these families and the broader social context.

COMING TO TERMS WITH A CHILD'S SPECIAL NEEDS

Most teachers have had significant losses or traumatic events in their lives, such as the death of someone close to them, and appreciate that these have involved them experiencing emotional reactions which were often surprising and sometimes quite frightening. They will also remember that these experiences sometimes led to them questioning their philosophical beliefs and values. Following major trauma or losses they will have been faced with new tasks or challenges. They will realize that we gradually learn to live with these major events in our lives, though they are not forgotten and feelings are re-triggered at various times in the future. They will also be aware that the way we react to such trauma is different for each individual.

Discovering that your child has special needs resulting from a serious illness, a disability or a psychological problem is a traumatic event for parents. In a way it represents a loss of the normal, healthy child they thought they had, coupled with uncertainty about many of their expectations for the future. For example, will their children be able to live a normal life, get a job, get married, or even be able to care for themselves well enough to be able to live away from the family home? The discovery that their child has special needs therefore generally leads to parents experiencing similar feelings and thoughts to those which are typical following any major trauma or loss. Four different models have been proposed to explain the process which parents experience in coming to terms with a child who has special needs. Each of these models explains a different aspect of the process and is therefore important in gaining a thorough understanding of what parents experience. The models to be described are ones which focus on stages of emotional reaction, a series of tasks or challenges, an examination of philosophical beliefs and values, and the re-experiencing of grief. These are discussed below.

Stages of emotional reaction

I have developed a model for the process of coming to terms with loss which I have found useful both for helping parents to talk about their reactions and feelings, and for increasing professional awareness of the process which parents may be going through. The model is similar to the stage model of mourning proposed by Kübler-Ross (1969) and stage models of adaptation to disability described by several writers (Bicknell, 1988; Gargiulo, 1985; Hornby, 1982; Seligman, 1979). In the model (presented in Figure 3.1) it is suggested that the process of adaptation to a significant loss can be viewed as a continuum of reactions, beginning at the time of the initial discovery of the loss, through which people pass in order to come to terms with it.

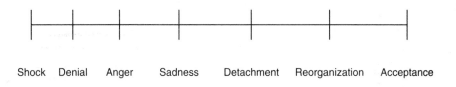

Shock   Denial   Anger   Sadness   Detachment   Reorganization   Acceptance

Figure 3.1 *Model for coming to terms with loss*

The visual representation of the model for coming to terms with loss illustrates the continuum of stages of reaction beginning with shock and passing through denial, anger, sadness, detachment and reorganization until the person achieves a mature emotional adjustment to the situation.

The initial reaction of most parents on being informed of their child's special needs is typically one of *shock*. Parents report feeling confusion, numbness, disorganization and helplessness and are typically unable to take in much of what they are told at this time. The shock reaction usually lasts from a few hours to a few days. When this reaction has subsided parents are more able to take in information and are generally keen to learn as much as they can about their child's condition and what can be done to help.

Shock is typically followed by a phase characterized by *denial* or disbelief of the reality of the situation. At first, many parents find it difficult to believe that their child has a problem. They may think that there must have been a mistake. It is understandable that they would want a second opinion and this option should be made available to them. However, for a few parents this leads to them 'shopping around' in an attempt to get a more favourable diagnosis, which, if found, will probably retard the adaptation process. This is why it is important that teachers are honest with parents and do not try to give them a prognosis which is too hopeful or unrealistic. Neither, of course, should they paint too bleak a picture. However, feedback from many parents has convinced me that the main qualities which they need from professionals at this time are accuracy and honesty. They want us to tell them exactly what we know and what we don't know. It is also very confusing for parents when professionals disagree about the diagnosis or prognosis and this can therefore reinforce their denial and retard the adaptation process.

As a temporary coping strategy, denial can be quite useful in giving parents time to adjust to the situation. It is only when denial is prolonged and intense that it is problematic. Some denial is probably present throughout the adaptation process and even when parents have apparently come to terms with their child's special needs there may still be an element of denial present. Teachers should therefore be sensitive to the degree to which parents will use denial to cope with their reactions to the loss. Teachers can help parents to overcome their use of denial by listening to them and sensitively providing them with objective information about their children's development and progress. Confronting the denial is seldom a useful strategy as it usually results in parents becoming anxious and rejecting the teacher rather than accepting the reality of the child's needs.

Following denial, when they are beginning to accept the reality of the situation, many parents experience *anger* about the loss. They may search for the cause of the problem or for someone to blame. If it is a chronic illness, then there may be an investigation of the family histories of both parents to find out whether there have been other members of the extended family who have had the same condition. If there is, then a parent's anger may be displaced on to their partner. Alternatively, underlying the anger may be feelings of guilt about somehow being responsible for their child's problem. For example, if it is a disability which has been caused by an accident parents may wonder what they could have done to prevent it occurring. Parents who experience anger as part of the adaptation process need to express it in order to move forward.

Teachers need not therefore take such anger personally or label parents as aggressive but they do need to be willing to encourage parents to express and explore their angry feelings.

Sadness typically follows anger and is a reaction which, more than any other, pervades the whole adaptation process. This sadness can be due to parents grieving for the loss of the healthy child which they thought they had, or it can be due to sadness about the loss of opportunities and ambitions which their children may not be able to fulfil. Either way, sadness, depression and, in some cases, even despair, are understandable reactions of parents to finding out that their child has a serious problem. Some parents have told me that they spent a lot of time crying. Others have reported that they felt so bad they couldn't face meeting anyone and tended to cut themselves off from social contact for a long time. For many parents sadness and depression are a normal part of the adaptation process. They must therefore not be labelled as depressive on the basis of experiencing this reaction for a period of time.

Following sadness parents typically experience a sort of *detachment*, when they feel empty and nothing seems to matter. Life goes on from day to day but it has lost its meaning. The appearance of this reaction is considered to indicate that the parent has begun to reluctantly accept the reality of the loss. It is therefore thought to be a turning-point in the adaptation process.

Reorganization is the reaction which follows detachment. It is characterized by realism about the situation and hope for the future. Parents begin to focus more on what their children may achieve and less on what they may miss out on. When parents have reached this stage they are typically more interested in participating in parent education programmes and joining support groups. So it is a good time to give parents the opportunity of attending parent programmes of various kinds. Being actively involved in facilitating their children's development and meeting up with other parents who have children with similar problems often helps parents to feel better about the whole situation and therefore is useful in helping parents make progress towards adaptation.

Finally, parents are considered to reach a point when they have come to terms with the situation and exhibit a mature emotional *acceptance* of their loss. They are fully aware of the child's special needs and strive to provide for these. However, children are treated, as much as possible, as just another member of the family, which does not revolve around them.

Of course, in reality, the adaptation process is not as clear cut as simply moving from stage to stage would suggest. One reaction may be uppermost at a particular time but certain amounts of the other reactions involved in the process will also be present. For example, when a person's main reaction is one of anger they will also be experiencing a fair amount of denial and sadness at the same time, and lesser amounts of the other reactions will also be present. Also, sadness and grief are considered to be the overriding feelings experienced and are ones which, more than any other, pervade all stages of the adaptation process.

Many parents say that they have experienced feelings associated with more than one stage at certain times. Some apparently did not experience a particular stage, while others report being fixated at one stage for a considerable time before being able to move on. Some people say that they experienced the stages in a different order. A few parents report that they are not aware of experiencing different reactions at different times. Thus, the process appears to be qualitatively different for each person.

Some parents may partially work through the adaptation process in anticipation of the loss. Confirmation of their child's problem by a professional is accompanied by feelings of relief for these parents. This appears to happen most often with parents of children with hearing impairment or specific learning difficulties, such as dyslexia, who have had difficulty getting professionals to make a definite diagnosis.

The adaptation process is considered to be a normal healthy reaction to the discovery of the child's problem and can be viewed as a form of grieving similar to that which follows any traumatic loss (Worden, 1991). Some parents appear to work through the process in a few days, whereas others seem to take years to reach a reasonable level of adaptation. It is generally considered that most people will take around two years to come to terms with any major loss such as diagnosis of a disability or serious illness. However, some parents seem to take longer and a few possibly never fully adjust to the situation.

Passage through the adaptation process can be accelerated or retarded by what parents do and by what professionals, such as teachers, say to them. Parents who refuse to accept their child's special needs and do not allow themselves to experience the feelings triggered by their loss will take much longer to come to terms with the situation. To use the terminology of grief therapy, parents need to do the 'grief work' associated with their loss in order to adjust to it (Worden, 1991).

Professionals can also slow down parents' progress through the adaptation process by being insensitive and thereby reinforcing parents' anger which can then become a fixation, since being angry is one way of avoiding facing up to the sadness associated with any loss. Passage through the adaptation process can also be retarded by professionals who suggest unrealistic prognoses which often result in parents becoming stuck in the denial stage, clinging on to unrealistic hopes of what their child might achieve.

Re-experiencing the grief

The fact that feelings associated with the loss can be re-triggered at various times in the future has led some writers to suggest that, rather than a grieving process which can be worked through with feelings to some extent resolved, parents of children with special needs experience 'chronic sorrow' (Olshansky, 1962; Wikler *et al.*, 1981). It is suggested that the reactions which are evoked such as anger, sadness and denial are not fully resolved but become an integral part of the parents' emotional life (Max, 1985). Thus, there will be various occasions when these reactions may be re-experienced. This reworking of parental reactions can occur at various transition points in the child's development, such as school entry, the onset of puberty, leaving school and leaving home (Wikler, 1981, 1986). It can also occur when parents are told about an additional problem at some time later than the original diagnosis. For example, Featherstone (1981) recounts how, having apparently come to terms with her child being blind, she was devastated when mental handicap was later diagnosed.

Examination of philosophical beliefs and values

Experiencing any serious trauma or major loss can lead to a person questioning their religious or ideological beliefs and rethinking the values which they hold most dear. Roos (1978), who is a parent of a child with a disability as well as being professionally involved in the disability field, suggests that many parents of children with special needs experience various fundamental existential conflicts. The existential conflicts identified by Roos include *disillusionment*. He considers that experience gradually erodes the high expectations which people develop as children, leading to disillusionment with ourselves, others, and life in general. Many people therefore channel their unrealistic expectations into their children. However, a child with special needs is usually an unsuitable vehicle for fulfilling these expectations and therefore can provoke a feeling of disillusionment.

Another conflict Roos calls *aloneness*. The fact that one is ultimately alone in one's passage through life is something that everyone must eventually come to terms with. Many people, however, attempt to avoid dealing with this conflict by establishing intimacy with their children. Since this may be more difficult to do with some children, for example those with learning difficulties or communication problems, parents are often forced to face up to their existential loneliness. *Vulnerability* occurs because as people mature they lose childhood fantasies of the omnipotence of their parents and themselves and begin to realise the tenuousness of their control over life, and therefore their personal vulnerability. Diagnosis of disability, serious illness or psychological disturbance in a member of the family can be a painful reminder of this vulnerability.

A conflict about *inequality* occurs because children grow up with the notion that fairness and justice ultimately prevail in life. Therefore, when faced with a child with special needs in the family, people may feel overwhelmed with the enormity of the apparent inequity, which can present a challenge to their ethical and religious beliefs. Also, maturity brings with it the realization of personal *insignificance*. Most people strive to find some meaning in life, typically through fulfilling satisfying social roles such as husband and father. When they are frustrated in achieving a rewarding parental role, perhaps because the child has a communication problem, parents may find it difficult to achieve meaning in their lives and therefore become vulnerable to feelings of insignificance.

Another conflict Roos terms *past orientation*. Thus, while most parents anticipate their children's future with enthusiasm, parents of children with special needs tend to view the future with apprehension. Hence, whereas most people are future oriented, such parents typically focus on the present or the past. Finally, he suggests that *loss of immortality* is another conflict. He explains that a common approach to coping with anxiety about one's own death is to seek symbolic immortality through one's children. When a child is disabled or has a serious illness, however, this potential avenue to immortality is threatened. Particularly when the child is an only child, parents may be forced to face up to this existential conflict.

Series of tasks and challenges

Another way in which the adaptation process can be viewed is to consider that it presents a number of challenges over and above those faced by people who have not experienced a major trauma or loss (Mitchell, 1985). Parents of children with special needs are seen as needing to address a series of tasks, each of which must be mastered at least partially if they are to come to terms with the situation. The major challenges and tasks for parents who have a child with a disability, chronic illness or psychological disturbance are listed below:

(1)   Parents must accept the reality of their child's special needs and come to terms with their own reactions to the situation

and to the reactions of family, friends and the wider community.

(2) Parents must gain an understanding of the nature of their child's special needs and learn skills for facilitating the child's development.

(3) Parents need to learn how to access relevant health, education and welfare services and establish working relationships with the professionals involved with their child.

(4) Parents need to learn how to participate appropriately in decision-making regarding their child's educational placement, medical treatment, future training and work placement.

(5) Parents need to identify individuals and groups who can provide them with support and to build up a support network.

(6) Parents must establish a positive parenting relationship and learn to cope with the day-to-day tasks of caring for their child with special needs.

(7) Parents must be able to maintain their self-esteem despite the difficulties they encounter, and maintain a positive relationship with their partner in order to establish a balanced family and personal life.

(8) Parents must be able to accept their children's right to independence, such as the expression of their sexuality and their need to live outside the family home.

(9) Parents must organize provision for their children with special needs for the future when they may become ill or die.

(10) Parents must be able to help the child understand his or her disability and adapt to living in the community.

Knowledge of the specific tasks which parents of children with special needs have to address enables practitioners to be aware of the kinds of issues which these parents may be dealing with, in addition to those of other parents, at various stages of the children's development. Further understanding which professionals need to develop in order to work effectively with parents involves knowledge of the ways in which families function, which is discussed in the following section.

EFFECTS ON AND OF FAMILY

Family systems perspective

Families are considered not only to be affected by children with special needs but also to have a significant impact on them (Bell, 1968; Mink and Nihira, 1987). Therefore, the type and severity of the child's illness, disability or psychological problem is likely to play an important role in how parents are affected. For example, a child with a serious illness will generally have a different impact on the family to a child with a disability. Likewise, a child with cancer will have a different impact to one with asthma and a child with a severe learning difficulty will affect the family differently to a child with dyslexia. In addition, the kind of people parents are will have an important bearing on the child's behaviour and development. Parents' personalities, coping strategies and the state of their health will all affect the child.

Also, as children with special needs pass through different developmental stages they will affect their families in different ways. For example, an infant with a disability or behaviour problem will have a different impact on parents from an adolescent with a similar condition. Likewise, the effect parents have on their child with special needs will depend on the particular stage in the life cycle which they are in. For example, a child who is the first-born child of young, recently married parents is in a very different position to a child with the same kind of special need who is born to older parents who already have several other children. The younger of these families is likely to experience higher levels of stress and have more difficulties in coping than the larger, more established family.

When teachers have children with special needs in their classes it is important for them not to lose sight of the fact that each child is a member of a family which will be affected by and affect the child. In fact, it is now believed that the behaviour of individual family members is strongly influenced by the functioning of the family system of which they are a part (Berger and Foster, 1986). Therefore, a change in the family system will inevitably lead to a change in the behaviour of each of the family members. For example, when one parent leaves the family home or dies all other family members will be affected and teachers can therefore expect to see changes in the behaviour of the children they have in their classes.

Likewise, a change in an individual's behaviour will cause the family dynamics to change. The implication of this is that what happens to a child with special needs at school will have an impact on the whole family to which that child belongs. Therefore, the whole family system needs to be taken into account when considering the effects of an intervention on an individual family member since the treatment of individual children, without taking their families into account, may result in an increase in problems experienced by the family as a whole (Chilman *et al.*, 1988). For example, the transfer of a child with special educational needs from a special school to a mainstream placement will affect not only the child but also other members of the family. A knowledge of family systems theory therefore provides an excellent rationale for teachers of children with special needs to always consider the child's family and, wherever possible, to work closely with parents in planning educational programmes.

Ecological model

It is now considered that human development and behaviour cannot be understood independently of the social context in which it occurs. The social environment influences the behaviour of children and families and this occurs at several levels. Thus, the effects on parents of caring for a child with any kind of special need are strongly influenced by the social environment in which they are living, including the extended family, services available and community attitudes. This is illustrated by the Ecological model of family functioning, adapted from that described by Bronfenbrenner (1979), which is presented in Figure 3.2. The model includes four different levels of influence on the family: the microsystem; the mesosystem; the exosystem; and the macrosystem.

Microsystem. The family of a child with a serious illness, disability or psychological problem is considered to constitute a *microsystem* with the child, parents and siblings reciprocally influencing each other. How well this nuclear family functions therefore depends on variables associated with each of its members.

(1) Features of the special need itself such as the type, severity and when it was diagnosed will have an influence. For example, a disability, such as a heart defect, which can be diagnosed shortly after birth can have a very different impact on the family to a learning difficulty which is usually not diagnosed until much later. It is generally considered that a special need which is diagnosed early in the child's life is easier to come to terms with than one that is diagnosed later, since parents will have believed for several months or even years that the child was normal in every way and may find it difficult to change this belief. The severity of the special need is also an important factor. A child with a severe learning difficulty is likely to have a different impact on the family from one who has a specific learning difficulty such as dyslexia. Also, uncertainties about the diagnosis which often occur with disabilities such as dyslexia, autism and mild to moderate levels of learning difficulty can be more difficult for families to come to terms with than in clear-cut cases such as Down's syndrome.

(2) Factors associated with the child with special needs and his or her siblings will have an influence on family functioning.

```
┌─────────────────────── MACROSYSTEM ───────────────────────┐
│                                                            │
│  Community        Culture           Ethnicity      Religion│
│                                                            │
│   ┌──────────────────── EXOSYSTEM ───────────────────┐     │
│   │                                                  │     │
│   │  Television/Radio/Newspapers – Health/Education/Welfare services │
│   │                                                  │     │
│   │   ┌──────────────── MESOSYSTEM ──────────────┐   │     │
│   │   │                                          │   │     │
│   │   │  Extended family/Friends/Colleagues/Neighbours/Other parents │
│   │   │                                          │   │     │
│   │   │   ┌────────── MICROSYSTEM ──────────┐    │   │     │
│   │   │   │  Special needs factors e.g. type/severity │    │     │
│   │   │   │                                 │    │   │     │
│   │   │   │  Child factors e.g. age/personality │ │   │     │
│   │   │   │                                 │    │   │     │
│   │   │   │  Sibling factors e.g. number/birth order │  │     │
│   │   │   │                                 │    │   │     │
│   │   │   │  Parent factors e.g. socioeconomic │  │   │     │
│   │   │   │         status/age/health/education │ │   │     │
│   │   │   └─────────────────────────────────┘    │   │     │
│   │   │                                          │   │     │
│   │   │  Teachers/Social workers/Psychologists/Therapists/Doctors │
│   │   │                                          │   │     │
│   │   └──────────────────────────────────────────┘   │     │
│   │                                                  │     │
│   │  Voluntary/Support groups   Recreation/Employment/Residential facilities │
│   │                                                  │     │
│   └──────────────────────────────────────────────────┘     │
│                                                            │
│  Economics              Politics            Legal system   │
│                                                            │
└────────────────────────────────────────────────────────────┘
```

Figure 3.2 *Ecological model of family functioning*

Whether the child is the first born, last born, a middle child, an only child or a twin will have an impact on the family. The ages and personalities of children and their siblings will also play a big part in how well the family functions. A young baby with a disability can be cute whereas the same child as an adolescent whose behaviour is difficult to manage can have quite a different effect on the family. Older siblings can be resentful of the attention given to the child with special needs and create problems of their own, or they can be helpful and make a substantial contribution to the family's well-being. Younger siblings can create extra worries for parents who often feel that they are unable to pay them sufficient attention.

(3)   Factors associated with the parents themselves and their relationship will have a major influence on family functioning. The parents' ages, personalities, socioeconomic status (SES), employment status, educational levels and the state of their health will all affect the family. For example, older parents are likely to have fewer financial worries than younger ones but may have more health problems of their own to worry about. Also, parents with extrovert personalities, who are optimistic and manage to keep a sense of humour, will typically experience less stress than those who tend to dwell on the negative aspects of the situation they find themselves in. In addition, a key factor in the functioning of the nuclear family is the quality of the parents' marriage. A healthy marital relationship will exert a positive influence on the family whereas the consequences of an unhappy marriage are likely to be tension and conflict throughout the family microsystem.

Mesosystem. The family microsystem is influenced by the mesosystem in which it is embedded. The mesosystem comprises the range of settings in which the family actively participates, such as the extended family and the community in which the family lives. The extended family has a key role in determining how well parents cope with having a child with special needs. If extended family members, such as the child's grandparents, are understanding and supportive they can have a significant positive influence on family functioning, whereas, if they are in conflict with the child's parents, or have little contact with them, the family misses out on an important potential source of support.

Neighbours, workmates, friends and other parents can also have a positive or negative influence on family functioning. When neighbours are friendly and allow the child with special needs into their homes to play with their own children parents can feel pleased that their family is accepted in the neighbourhood. If neighbours are unfriendly then this can put an added strain on to the family. Workmates and managers can also have an influence on the family. For example, managers who are prepared to give parents time off work to attend important appointments concerning their children can reduce parents' stress levels and thereby contribute positively to family well-being. In contrast, workmates who talk of their own children's achievements while being too embarrassed to talk about the child with special needs turn a possible source of support into one of tension and unhappiness.

Typically, some of the parents' friends will find it difficult to adjust to them having a child with special needs and will tend to stay away. Parents themselves often shy away from many of their previous friends when they discover that their child has a serious illness, disability or psychological problem. This reduces the possible sources of support for the family. However, when parents meet up with other parents of children with similar difficulties they often form friendships which are very supportive and long-lasting. In many cases these friendships form an invaluable source of support for families.

The contacts which parents have with, for example, social workers, teachers and doctors can help to promote healthy family functioning if these professionals are sensitive, understanding, knowledgeable and supportive. Parents of children with special needs generally have a great deal of contact with professionals in the health, education and social welfare fields who can be an invaluable source of support and guidance, for example, regarding appropriate therapy, services and financial assistance. However, when parents find contacts with workers to be unhelpful, or even aversive, this increases stress and leads to reduced feelings of well-being within the family. *See previous statements p.40*

Exosystem. The mesosystem is itself influenced by the exosystem which consists of social settings which indirectly affect the family, such as the mass media, education system and voluntary agencies:

(1)   The way children with special needs are portrayed in the newspapers or on television will have an impact on the family. For example, when stereotyped and patronizing attitudes toward people with disabilities are perpetuated by the media this does not help families who have disabled members to integrate into the community.

(2)   The quality and types of health, education and social welfare services available to parents will have a critical influence on the way in which these families cope with their child's special needs. This is made clear when families with disabled children

in developing countries, such as India, are considered. In many cases of severe disability such children do not attend school, no financial assistance is available to parents and medical attention is inadequate at best. Families in this situation will clearly find life very difficult indeed. Although the picture in Western countries, such as England, is generally much better, current political influences are forcing education, health and welfare services to operate like businesses. This is likely to have negative consequences for families of children with disabilities who typically need more intensive levels of help in these areas. For example, the availability of respite care for children with disabilities, so that families can have a break from time to time, is critical in helping many families cope. If the availability of this temporary care is reduced then this will have a negative impact on the functioning of many families.

(3) The availability of various voluntary societies and support groups which have been established to help the parents of children with special needs can be a significant factor in determining how well these families cope. Many cities in the UK now have branches of the major voluntary societies such as MENCAP and an abundance of local support groups. For example, in Hull, which is a city of about 300,000 people, the local newspaper has a helplines column which lists support groups focused on a wide variety of special needs, including autism; Down's syndrome; child abuse; cot death; mental illness; bereavement; and stepfamilies.

(4) The availability of recreation facilities, in the local community, suitable for the participation of children with special needs is very important in helping families cope. For example, institutions such as sports and leisure centres can ensure that they provide appropriate access and programmes for people with disabilities of various kinds. However, many parents find that recreational activities suitable for their children or young adults with disabilities in their local communities are inadequate, which results in these young people being bored at home for much of their free time and an additional strain being put on the family.

(5) The employment and residential opportunities available for adults who have a chronic illness or disability has an indirect effect on how families function. One of the most frequently mentioned concerns of parents who have children with special needs is anxiety about what will happen to their children in the future. In communities where there are various employment and residential options for young adults with such difficulties parents' worries are minimized. When this is

not the case an enormous strain is placed on parents in attempting to find suitable work and living arrangements for when their children leave school.

Macrosystem. Finally, there is the macrosystem which refers to the attitudes, beliefs, values and ideologies inherent in the social institutions of a particular society, which all have an impact on the way a family of a child with special needs will function. First of all, the particular culture in which the family is living will have major effects on the family. If the culture is one which emphasizes humanitarian values then there are much more likely to be positive attitudes towards people with chronic illness, disability or psychological problems than in cultures which emphasize materialism. Also, the specific type of society in which the family lives will have an impact on many different aspects of family life. For example, if the family lives in a rural community in a developing country then it may be easier to prepare a child with special needs for the types of work which are available than if the family lives in an urban community in an industrialized country.

The beliefs of the particular ethnic group to which the family belongs will exert an influence on the way the family reacts to the child's special needs. For example, there is a belief held by some people in traditional Samoan society that having a disabled child in the family is the result of the father being unfaithful to his wife, so that the child brings shame on the family. Religious beliefs also have a part to play in how families cope with having a disabled member. If the family believes the disabled child to be a gift of God then it will be much easier for them to accept the situation than if the disability is seen as a form of punishment for some sin which has been committed. Another example is that some traditional Hindu families in India place more store in going to the temple to make a gift to the Gods than they do in organizing therapy for the child.

The overall economic situation in the society in which the family lives will affect many aspects of how the family copes with having a child with special needs. Typically, in developing countries, where there is insufficient money available to provide essential health and education services to the community, many of the facilities which are available for children with special needs have been established by charitable organizations and a large proportion of such children do not receive appropriate health care, therapy or education. The professional guidance and financial support that is available to families in developed countries will also be mainly lacking in developing countries, which adds to the difficulties experienced by these families.

In countries which are better off economically, political policies will be instrumental in determining how the resources are distributed. When economic policies are more concerned with increasing profits than with improving the quality of life of the citizens, then families who have members with special needs are likely to do less well. The political system in each country is responsible for the legislation regarding the rights of children with special needs and their families. The legal system has a role to play in interpreting the law in terms of individual cases of children with special needs. However, these cases typically indirectly affect large numbers of similar families since the legal rulings are often used to provide guidance for services in the health, education and social welfare fields. Recent years have witnessed increasing use of the legal systems in countries such as the USA and the UK by parents attempting to ensure their children with special needs receive the best possible services. The ability to engage in such a process is clearly important in determining the levels of support available to such families.

In conclusion, it must now be clear that how a family which has a member with special needs functions is influenced, not only by interactions within the family's microsystem but also by its interactions with other levels of the entire social system, which all need to be taken into account by professionals when they are working with children with special needs and their families.

SUMMARY AND CONCLUSIONS

Teachers of children with special needs should be aware of the likely impact of caring for such children on members of their families. An understanding of the process by which parents and other family members adapt or come to terms with a child's illness, disability or psychological problem is therefore essential. Models for the adaptation process which have been discussed include ones which view it as comprising: stages of emotional reaction; a series of tasks or challenges; an examination of philosophical beliefs and values; and the re-experiencing of grief. Also essential is an understanding of the ways in which these families are affected by having a child with special needs. Family functioning is considered from the perspective of family systems theory and an ecological model which takes into account the influence of the social environment in which families live. It is proposed that if teachers are to establish productive working relationships with parents then they need to have a comprehensive knowledge of the issues addressed in this chapter.

The following chapter considers the effects on families of four different types of special needs resulting from children's disabilities and medical conditions, and from the impact of parental separation and bereavement on children.

4

Helping parents of children with various special needs

INTRODUCTION

During my first few months of working as an educational psychologist in New Zealand I was asked to see a 4-year-old girl who was causing concern at the kindergarten she attended. The problem was that Meeka became hysterical whenever her mother attempted to leave the kindergarten. The teachers had done all they could to distract Meeka and involve her in activities with the other children but she would just sit and cry until her mother returned. After observing Meeka while the teachers once more tried unsuccessfully to keep her attention while her mother slipped away I wondered if the problem was something more than simple separation anxiety. I therefore decided to see Meeka again but this time at my office so that I could observe her further, talk to her mother and do a developmental assessment.

Results of the assessment, observations of Meeka's behaviour and a developmental check-list completed by questioning her mother all suggested that Meeka was functioning intellectually at around a 2-year-old level. Thus, her development was found to be significantly delayed and she fell within the range for which children could be considered for placement in special pre-school facilities for children categorized in New Zealand as 'intellectually handicapped'. I discussed this possibility with Meeka's mother who agreed to visit some of the special facilities for which she was eligible. I arranged for us to visit three special pre-schools which were within reasonable travelling distance of the family home.

On the appointed day I collected Meeka, her mother and her maternal grandmother from their home and we set off to investigate the three schools. We talked to staff and observed children in the first two schools while Meeka clung on to her mother, who clearly had some reservations about each of them. At the third school, as the adults talked, Meeka left her mother to play on the equipment with the other children. After a few minutes it was clear that she was having a wonderful time and fitted in perfectly. Mother and grandmother were convinced, after talking to the headteacher and seeing Meeka fit in so well, that this was the place for her. The headteacher said that a place was available so she could start on the following Monday. Meeka actually cried when her mother went to take her back to the car – she wanted to stay and play.

I dropped everyone back home and went back to the office to do the necessary paperwork. I think I was still slapping myself on the back for a job well done at Monday lunchtime when the headteacher of the special pre-school phoned our office. She told us that Meeka's father had just been to visit and had withdrawn her because he 'didn't want his daughter going to a school for handicapped kids'!

I had made two very important mistakes. First, I had seen Meeka's mother several times and even met grandmother but I had never talked with father, either about the results of the assessment or about her placement in a special pre-school. I had overlooked the fact that most children have two parents who are both concerned about their education and care. Second, I had also not realized that by passing on the assessment results and by suggesting the special pre-school placement I was effectively diagnosing a severe learning difficulty in a child whose parents had apparently not considered the possibility that their child had any sort of disability.

What I should have done, as soon as possible after I did the assessment, was to arrange a meeting with both parents to discuss the results. This should have been done in private, with Meeka present. I should have explained the possible implications of the results as sensitively and objectively as I could and given her parents the opportunity to absorb all this and ask any questions they wanted to. I should have been prepared to provide the parents with up-to-date information about the disability and the various services and voluntary agencies which could be of help to them. I should have been ready to help the parents consider the various options for Meeka's educational placement. Finally, I should have been sensitive to the fact that her parents might not have been able to take all this in during one meeting and would need further meetings in order to come to terms with the situation and plan effectively for Meeka.

But I did none of these things because I never arranged to see Meeka's father. The consequences of this were that her parents were left to struggle with the implications of the diagnosis of their daughter's disability which caused considerable distress for them and other members of the family. Fortunately, Meeka's mother had involved her own mother in attempting to sort out her granddaughter's difficulties and in visiting the special pre-schools. I understand that it was she who persuaded her son-in-law to allow Meeka to return to the school a few days later.

This case taught me the importance for teachers and other professionals in the field of education of considering the effects of a child's special needs on the whole family. When a child has a serious illness or disability it affects not only the parents but also other members of the family such as siblings and grandparents as well as friends and sometimes other members of their communities as well. Similarly, when children are coping with the death of a family member or the divorce of their parents, their reactions are likely to have an impact on their families. In addition, their behaviour and progress at school may be affected.

This chapter considers the effects on families, and their members, of disability, medical conditions, bereavement and divorce and provides guidelines for teachers in their work with parents whose families are experiencing each of these potentially traumatic situations.

CHILDREN WITH DISABILITIES

Children with disabilities make up the largest group of children with special needs to be found in schools. The Warnock Report (DES, 1978) estimated that approximately one in six children would have special educational needs (SEN) throughout their school lives and one in five, or 20 per cent, would have such needs at some stage in their schooling. The largest proportion of children with SEN are those with mild learning difficulties who are sometimes referred to as slow learners, the vast majority of whom are educated in ordinary schools. Three other large groups of children with SEN are those with specific learning difficulties (dyslexia), moderate learning difficulties and emotional or behavioural difficulties (EBD). Of these three groups the majority of children with EBD and specific learning difficulties are educated in ordinary schools. Children with moderate learning difficulties, most of whom used to be educated in special schools, are being integrated into mainstream schools in increasing numbers. Children with physical disabilities, hearing impairment and visual impairment make up only a small proportion of the population of pupils with SEN but are also being integrated into ordinary schools in increasing numbers. Therefore, teachers in mainstream schools are likely to have several pupils, possibly with different types of SEN, in each of their ordinary classes. Because of this, teachers need to be aware of the effects of children with disabilities on their families and to be able to work effectively with their parents.

Effects on families

More research has focused on the effects on families which have members with disabilities than any other type of special need. The findings of this research are therefore presented in some detail in order to illustrate the wide-ranging effects on families of having a child with special needs.

Mothers Most of the research which has been conducted with parents of children with disabilities has focused on mothers and has shown that the bulk of the housework and child care in such families is carried out by them (Fewell and Vadasy, 1986). Despite the increased demands which a child with a disability makes on these aspects of family life fathers generally do not make a bigger contribution than they make in ordinary families (McConachie, 1986). This may at least partially account for the fact that mothers of disabled children have been consistently found to have higher levels of stress and a higher incidence of stress-related physical and mental disorders than mothers of non-disabled children (Minnes, 1988). Mothers tend to be the ones who take children to their various appointments and have more contact with professionals, so having more opportunities to discuss their child's disability with them than fathers. Mothers also tend to have more contact with sources of support such as other mothers of children with similar disabilities, friends and family members. These factors are likely to help mothers to move through the adaptation process which may lead to fathers experiencing greater difficulties than mothers in coming to terms with their children's disability.

Fathers Since most fathers go off to work during the day and generally have other interests outside the home their mental health may be less threatened than that of mothers by having a child with a disability. However, it is suggested that some fathers use denial in order to avoid facing up to the full extent of the disability or to hide their true feelings about the situation. This is illustrated by the story of Stephen's father which was discussed in Chapter 1.

In fact, the overall impression gained from the literature about effects on fathers of parenting children with disabilities is generally a negative one. For example, fathers are often reported to have difficulty in accepting their child's disability, particularly if it occurs in a son or if the child is severely handicapped (Lamb, 1983). Also, fathers are reported to experience a higher level of depression, personality difficulties and marital relationship problems than fathers of non-disabled children (Meyer, 1986a, 1986b). However, a recent detailed analysis of the literature found that the negative comments about fathers were based on very little hard data (Hornby, 1994a). Also, a recent study conducted by the author found little evidence for these negative effects on fathers. The 100 fathers of children with Down's syndrome, who were interviewed and completed questionnaires, were found not to differ significantly from other fathers on the variables studied, such as stress, depression, personality factors and levels of marital satisfaction (Hornby, 1995a, 1995b).

Marital relationships Much has been written concerning the potential marital difficulties faced by parents of children with disabilities (e.g. Featherstone, 1981). These difficulties are considered to be related to the additional demands of caring for a child with a disability, and various other factors. For example, it is suggested that partners may disagree about the child's care or treatment and have insufficient time to resolve their conflicts. Having to deal with several professionals may increase the strain on parents, particularly since it is usually the mother who meets the professionals, and who has to reinterpret these meetings for the father. Also, as suggested above, because of greater involvement with professionals, the child and sources of support, mothers sometimes move through the adaptation process more quickly than fathers, creating another potential area for conflict. Difficulties in sexual relationships may result from a lack of privacy, fatigue, a sense of isolation on the part of each spouse, or the fear of producing another disabled child.

The prevalence of marriage breakdown in such families has been the subject of considerable research. Early studies reported finding increased marriage breakdown and low marital satisfaction (e.g. Gath, 1977; Tew *et al.*, 1974) but more recent studies have generally found average levels of marital satisfaction and breakdown (Gath and Gumley, 1984; Hornby, 1995b; Roesel and Lawlis, 1983). An important and consistent finding is that a stable and satisfying marriage appears to reduce the stress experienced by parents in coping with a disabled child (Minnes, 1988). Some writers have suggested that having a child with a disability in the family tends to strengthen strong marriages and weaken fragile ones (Brotherson *et al.*, 1986).

Family life The social life of many families with disabled members is likely to be restricted in one way or another (Lonsdale, 1978). Leisure activities such as participation in sports and other clubs and family activities, such as visiting friends, having picnics and attending family gatherings, are often affected. Many families are restricted in the use they can make of community facilities such as beaches, restaurants and public transport. There are also limitations on the type of holidays which families can take. The extent of the social restriction is greatest when the children are young, when physical handicap or behavioural problems are present and when the degree of disability is severe (Gallagher *et al.*, 1983).

Families who have children with disabilities are also likely to have to meet additional expenses (Murphy, 1982). These are most often for medical care, clothing and transport. The family's income may also be reduced since one parent is prevented from going out to work because of the daily care requirements of the disabled child (McAndrew, 1976). Most developed countries have various financial benefits available to assist such families. However, surveys have shown that many parents do not receive the benefits to which they are entitled (Philip and Duckworth, 1982).

Siblings Much has been written about the possible harmful effects on the siblings of children with disabilities, both by professionals (Meyer *et al.*, 1985a; Seligman and Darling, 1989) and by parents themselves (Klein and Schleifer, 1993). It is suggested that there are several factors which can contribute to sibling maladjustment. Siblings may be given excessive caring responsibilities or may feel the need to overachieve to compensate for parental disappointment with the disabled child. Children may also wonder whether parents will expect them to care for their disabled sibling in later life and may worry about finding a partner who would be willing to share such a responsibility. Other common concerns are anxiety about 'catching' the disability or about the future possibility of producing children with disabilities themselves (Simeonsson and McHale, 1981).

Siblings may feel isolated because their brother or sister is unable to share many of the experiences of growing up. This feeling is compounded by the family being somewhat cut off from the community because of the child with the disability. For example, siblings may feel embarrassed about their brother or sister and avoid bringing friends home, which may have a negative impact on their friendship network. Or they may feel resentment about the extra time and attention which parents give to their brother or sister with a disability. Siblings may feel guilty about their embarrassment or resentment or about feeling angry. They may also feel guilty simply because their brother or sister has a disability and they do not. Finally, such feelings are often compounded by the fact that siblings typically avoid seeking support from their parents since they feel that they have enough to cope with already (Powell and Ogle, 1992).

There are, however, several reports of the positive effects on sibling adjustment of having a disabled family member. One example of this is that many siblings are reported to choose careers in the helping professions such as teaching or social work (Crnic and Leconte, 1986). Other researchers have suggested that siblings of children with disabilities tend to be more insightful and tolerant of others' difficulties, to be more certain of their goals in life, to demonstrate greater social competence, and to develop a maturity beyond their years (Ferrari, 1984; Grossman, 1972).

Grandparents A common source of support for the family may be the child's grandparents. Grandparents can provide emotional support, guidance about child care, access to community resources, as well as help with shopping, babysitting and financial support (Sonnek, 1986). However, some reports have suggested that many grandparents have difficulty adapting to the situation and attempt either to deny the reality of the disability or to reject the child (George, 1988). Another reported problem is the paternal grandmother's resentment of her daughter-in-law for not producing a normal child (Pieper, 1976). These difficulties can lead to a breakdown in the relationship between parents and grandparents, which is then likely to have a pervasive effect on family members. In fact, a recent survey of parents of children with severe learning difficulties found that there was a low level of support from grandparents (Hornby and Ashworth, 1994). A minority of grandparents provided a high level of support. More support was received from maternal grandparents than paternal grandparents. However, generally, grandparents were found to provide minimal support for the families caring for their disabled grandchildren.

What teachers can do to help

It is clear from the foregoing discussion that a child with a disability affects all other family members to some extent as well as having an impact on the parents' relationship with one another and family life in general. It is therefore important for teachers and other professionals who work with children with disabilities not to consider them in isolation but to take into account the entire family system of which they are a part, as noted in Chapter 3 and elaborated below.

Consider whole family's needs It is important for teachers to remember that any intervention they implement with a child with a disability will affect other members of the child's family, in particular the parents. So the impact of any intervention, such as a change of class or a home–school programme, on the wider family should be considered before it is implemented. In addition, the teacher needs to be concerned with the welfare of all family members and must be prepared to help parents deal with difficulties which they and other family members are experiencing that are related to caring for a child with a disability. For example, parents should be informed about the support groups and workshops (discussed in Chapter 8) which they, or other family members, would benefit from attending.

Maintain two-way communication The most important way in which teachers can be of help to parents is for them to establish and maintain effective two-way communication between home and school. In this way any learning or behavioural difficulties which children experience can be dealt with quickly by teacher and parent working together. In addition, any other concerns which parents have about family members, or that teachers have about any aspects of the child's schooling, can be discussed openly and appropriate steps taken. Maintaining contact with parents by means of telephone calls, meetings and various written forms of communication is discussed in detail in Chapter 6.

Sensitive communication of the results of assessments and reviews Parents of children with disabilities often experience considerable anxiety about assessments and reviews of progress conducted with their children. They, therefore, need to be told assessment results, or be given a progress report, by a teacher who communicates empathy, sensitivity, openness and a constructive outlook. Parents prefer to meet with teachers as soon as possible after an assessment is conducted or a difficulty the child is having at school becomes apparent. Most parents prefer for both of them to attend such meetings and to have adequate time for asking questions.

Providing information Parents need to have comprehensive, accurate and up-to-date information about the child's disability. Most parents also want suggestions about what they can do to facilitate the child's development. Many parents are interested in participating in some form of home–school intervention programme of the kind described in Chapter 7. Parents should also be informed about all the services and benefits available to help them care for their children. This information is widely available in the form of both written materials and professional knowledge (Stone and Taylor, 1977). It is therefore quite alarming to discover how often it does not get to the people who need it. Teachers should therefore always check that parents have all the information they need about their child's disability and that they know about the relevant agencies and support groups which operate in their community. Making sure that parents know about the various grants and government benefits for which they are eligible is particularly important.

Providing support Parents and other family members need to have supportive counselling available to them from the diagnosis of disability onwards. In many cases this is provided by members of the extended family, or friends or by other parents who have children with disabilities. But teachers also need to be able to provide support. Parents are seldom willing to seek counselling for themselves whereas they will ask teachers about concerns they have about their children. This then provides an opportunity for teachers to use the listening and counselling skills, which are described in Chapter 5, to deal with any other concerns parents may have and thereby facilitate their movement through the adaptation process, which was discussed in Chapter 3.

Linking family members with others in similar circumstances Most parents want to meet others who have children with similar disabilities. Although many parents wish to do this as soon as a disability is diagnosed, some do not want such meetings for several months or even years. When parents do meet others who have children with similar disabilities they typically gain substantial benefits both in terms of receiving emotional support and in obtaining information, such as about benefits available and respite care (Featherstone, 1981). Other family members, such as siblings and grandparents, also gain greatly from meeting with their peers from other exceptional families (see Chapter 8). Teachers can help to facilitate these contacts by making families aware of the various support groups and other disability organizations operating in their area.

CHILDREN WITH MEDICAL CONDITIONS

> Children with identified medical needs will not necessarily have an associated learning difficulty, but the consequences of their illness or condition may lead to future difficulties if there is not close collaboration between the school, the relevant child health services and parents. (DFE, 1994, p. 18)

This quotation from the *Code of Practice on the Identification and Assessment of Special Educational Needs* reinforces the importance for teachers of considering the needs of children with various medical conditions. As suggested in the quotation, if appropriate help is not provided for such children then they are likely to develop learning difficulties or emotional and behavioural difficulties. It is therefore important to ensure that the special needs of these children are met so that such difficulties do not occur.

A wide variety of chronic and life-threatening illnesses are found among children in mainstream schools (Lansdown, 1980). The most common of these is probably asthma with at least one in twenty children affected to some extent by this condition. Other common childhood diseases are eczema, diabetes, heart defects, epilepsy and rheumatoid arthritis. Medical conditions which are less common but which are often found in mainstream schools include cystic fibrosis, leukaemia, muscular dystrophy, kidney disease, haemophilia, sickle cell anaemia and phenylketonuria (PKU).

Teachers in mainstream schools are likely to have one or more pupils, with different medical conditions, in each of their classes. Therefore, teachers need to be aware of the effects of such illnesses on children themselves and on their families, and to be able to collaborate with parents in meeting the children's special needs.

Effects on children

Children with chronic or life-threatening illnesses may have associated special needs for several reasons (Eiser, 1993). Children with conditions such as epilepsy or asthma may require drug treatment which can make them drowsy or impair their concentration. Children with life-threatening conditions such as heart disease, cancer, brain tumours or cystic fibrosis may need frequent hospital treatment. This necessitates them having considerable time off school which makes it difficult for them to maintain satisfactory progress. Also, the treatment required for some of these conditions involves chemotherapy or radiotherapy which typically leaves children feeling quite ill. Other chronic conditions such as eczema and rheumatoid arthritis may be painful and therefore deplete children's reserves of energy so that they cannot continue to work for long periods of time. They need more breaks in order to cope with fatigue. Finally, in dealing with children with serious illnesses, teachers may place more emphasis on social development and lower their academic expectations of children. Thus, all these medical conditions can have a negative impact on children's academic attainment.

In addition, suffering from a medical condition is likely to have a psychological impact on children. They may feel different from their peers and sometimes experience teasing or rejection because of their illness (Eiser, 1993). This can happen to children whose treatment has led to changes in their appearance, such as hair loss in the treatment of cancers. It can also happen to children whose illness prevents them from taking part in normal activities with their peers, such as children with cystic fibrosis who need to spend most of their lunchtime receiving physiotherapy. Children may also have fears or anxieties about their illness which they are unable to express. Or they may find it difficult to cope with the additional demands which their illness places on them, such as injecting themselves with insulin in the case of diabetics, or the restriction of their diet in PKU. Therefore, the psychological impact of such conditions can lead to children experiencing emotional or behavioural difficulties.

Effects on families

Children with chronic or life-threatening illnesses can be a major source of stress for their parents and other members of their families. Researchers have reported higher levels of stress and associated psychological problems in such families (e.g. Burton, 1974, 1975; Eiser, 1993). In many ways the effects on the family, including parents, siblings and grandparents, are similar to those found for children with disabilities, which were discussed earlier in this chapter. In general, the adaptation of family members to a child with a medical condition tends not to be related to the type or severity of the illness. Family adaptation is more clearly related to the social and emotional support available, parental health (both mental and physical), the quality of the marital relationship, and other family variables such as open communication, ability to express emotions, family cohesiveness, family stability, and the level of conflict within the family (Davis, 1993).

What teachers can do to help

The school has a very important part to play in the overall development of children who suffer chronic or life-threatening illnesses. Parents typically look to schools to provide a haven of normality for children whose lives are disrupted by their illnesses. Therefore, regardless of the severity of the illness it is generally best to ensure that children's experience of school is as normal as possible. Eiser (1993) reports on research which suggests that the role of the teacher is vital in the successful integration of children with medical conditions into schools. In this regard, parents particularly appreciated several qualities in teachers. First, they valued teachers who exhibited a caring attitude towards their child. Second, they appreciated teachers who treated their child as normally as possible. Third, they rated highly teachers who gave their children additional help with their work. Fourth, they especially valued teachers who kept them well informed about what was happening in the classroom.

It is essential that parents, teachers and health care professionals establish a working partnership in order to ensure that children's medical needs are met within an environment which is kept as normal as possible. To this end, Wadsworth *et al.* (1993) have suggested guidelines for teachers working with parents of children who have chronic or life-threatening illnesses. These are summarized below.

Establishing communication Teachers need to establish effective two-way communication with parents in order to collaborate in resolving any difficulties which occur at school or at home. Parents should feel able to contact teachers about problems they are having at home. Likewise, teachers should feel able to seek parents' help in resolving any difficulties which occur at school. Strategies for achieving such two-way communication are discussed in Chapter 6.

Developing empathy Teachers need to develop an understanding of the perspective of parents who have children with medical conditions and of the children themselves. It is important to take the time to develop rapport with the children and their parents. Teachers can help children to fit into class activities in ways which minimize the distractions caused by their medical needs. They need to be patient when dealing with parents' anxieties concerning their children and in encouraging parents to develop their children's independence and relationships outside the family.

Making home visits Most parents appreciate teachers who are willing to make home visits in order to learn as much as possible about the child's medical condition. Home visits are also useful in developing rapport with parents who typically enjoy the opportunity of meeting with teachers in the more relaxed environment of their own home. Additionally, home visits enable teachers to assess home circumstances and observe children interacting with their parents. The information gained from these observations is often invaluable in planning to meet a child's special needs at school. Strategies for making successful home visits are discussed in Chapter 6.

Obtaining information from parents Teachers need to ensure that they have obtained as much information as possible from parents about their children's medical conditions and related special needs. Information about children's medical needs is of primary importance but it will also be useful to find out about children's likes and dislikes concerning such things as food and play activities. Finding out about any fears which children have and methods for managing their behaviour which are used at home will also be useful.

Liaison with health service personnel Teachers need to liaise closely with health care professionals responsible for the children in their classes with chronic or life-threatening illnesses. Effective communication between teachers, parents and medical personnel is clearly crucial in ensuring the child's medical needs are met. Teachers may also need to be flexible in organizing classroom activities to take into account a child's medical requirements. They should be prepared to accept guidance or in-service training from health service personnel regarding such things as the administration of medication and the operation of special equipment. However, teachers cannot be expected to supervise extensive medical treatment at school. This must be the domain of qualified medical personnel.

Developing contingency plans Teachers need to collaborate with parents in developing contingency plans for various situations which may arise. For example, what should the teacher do if the child becomes ill at school? What should the teacher do if essential equipment breaks down or if there is a power failure? Contingency plans for all such situations need to be written down and filed away ready for easy access by school staff.

Facilitating peer acceptance Teachers will need to educate the rest of the child's class, and possibly other members of staff, about the child's medical condition. They can also facilitate peer acceptance of the child by such means as assigning the child 'buddies' or by using co-operative learning activities (Johnson and Johnson, 1987).

Designing individual education plans Teachers should ensure that parents and health care personnel are fully involved in designing the child's Individual Education Plan (IEP) as well as in regular reviews of the child's progress. Strategies for facilitating parental involvement in the development of IEPs and reviews are discussed in Chapter 7. For a child with a serious medical condition it is also important to obtain appropriate participation of health care professionals in the IEP and review processes.

Ensuring availability of support Teachers need to ensure that parents are aware of the availability of sources of practical and emotional support for themselves and other family members. As discussed in Chapter 3, there is now a wide range of professional and voluntary agencies and groups offering support to families who have a child with special needs. An important function which teachers can fulfil for such parents is to find out whether parents have established a support network for their families and to alert parents to sources of support which they are not aware of. Teachers themselves are, of course, an important part of this network and therefore need to develop the listening and counselling skills discussed in Chapter 5.

Considering the entire class Whereas parents' concern is understandably mainly for the welfare of their children, teachers must view the needs of the child who is ill within the context of the whole class. Meeting the special needs of such children cannot be allowed to jeopardize the education of the other children in the class.

CHILDREN COPING WITH BEREAVEMENT

Census figures show that approximately 650,000 people die in the UK each year. It is estimated that over 1.5 million people will suffer a major bereavement because of these deaths and that at any time around 180,000 children under the age of 16 will grow up having lost a parent through death. In addition, many children will experience the death of a sibling or another close family member such as a grandparent. Others will have to cope with the loss of a close friend or someone they know less well, but who is nevertheless significant to them, such as a classmate or teacher.

It is clear that experiencing the death of someone close to them is a common occurrence for children. However, it is one which is generally paid insufficient attention by parents and teachers. This is largely because most people know very little about children's reactions to death or how to help them cope with bereavement, so they tend to avoid the issue. The result of this is that many children have problems coming to terms with their losses.

The emotional and behavioural difficulties which are often experienced by children in coping with bereavement were first systematically studied by Rutter (1966) who found that twice as many children who had lost a parent by death attended the Maudsley Hospital psychiatric clinic than would be expected from death rates in the general population. He also found that about 14 per cent of children attending a child guidance clinic had been bereaved of a close relative in the recent past. Rutter observed a variety of problems in children who had been bereaved including anti-social behaviour, depression and various phobias.

More recently, Morgan (1985) has reviewed the literature on children's reactions to death and provides the following list of possible responses:

• regression to an earlier stage of development

- hostile reactions to the deceased
- hostile reactions to others
- eating disorders
- bedwetting
- sleep disturbances
- other psychosomatic disorders
- attempting to replace the deceased
- adopting the mannerisms of the deceased
- aggressive behaviour
- discipline problems
- learning difficulties
- denial
- withdrawal
- guilt
- anxiety
- panic.

Children's difficulties in coping with bereavement

Three cases of children whose difficulties in coping with a bereavement came to light at school will serve as illustrations of the possible ways children may react. The first was a 14-year-old boy who had been suspended from school for being disruptive and for using abusive language to a teacher. This kind of behaviour was uncharacteristic for this pupil so the school asked me, as their educational psychologist, to interview him and report to the governors on whether he should be reinstated or expelled. In the course of the interview it emerged that the boy's grandfather, whom he had been very close to, had recently died. He was clearly very upset and confused about this and had not had the chance to talk to anyone about it. When I passed on this information to the school governors they agreed to take him back and assigned a teacher he knew well to be available for him to talk to. His parents also said they would make sure that the family would help the boy to cope with his loss. Apparently, his uncharacteristic disruptive behaviour at school had been a cry for help.

The second case was of a 10-year-old blind boy who was referred to the Psychological Service in which I worked because he was having very bad dreams and was beginning to have problems sleeping. On talking with him it emerged that the teacher who had taught him Braille for the past five years had recently died. Since this had happened during the summer holidays none of the children had gone to her funeral. So when school restarted he suddenly had a new Braille teacher and hardly anything was said about what happened to the previous one. This he had found very frightening and it appeared to be what accounted for his bad dreams and sleeping problems. He badly needed to explore his feelings and fantasies about the death of his teacher but had not been given the opportunity to do this. I explained the situation to the boy's mother (who came with him for the appointment) and suggested that both parents and the teachers at school should talk with him about the Braille teacher's death. When the boy returned to see me the following week the bad dreams and sleep problems had disappeared.

The third case is of a 13-year-old boy who is currently a member of a friend of mine's form class. Almost two years ago my friend told me that the boy was upset because he had learned that his father was dying of cancer. The father died shortly afterwards. Since that time the boy's behaviour at school has seriously deteriorated with frequent incidents of disruptive or bizarre behaviour. He has also been very difficult at home and his mother is finding it very hard to cope with him. My friend tells me that at no time has the boy or his mother been offered any counselling to help him or other family members to cope with the bereavement.

In my experience these cases are fairly typical of the way in which teachers and parents handle bereavement in children. People are not sure what to do, so they do nothing! When the death of a parent or child occurs it affects all members of the family. Parents may be struggling to cope themselves and therefore may not be able to give grieving children the help they need. Parents also may not be aware of children's understanding of death or of the likely effects of bereavement on children. Most importantly, parents may not know what can be done to help children to cope. To make matters worse children are often aware that their parents are upset following the death and tend to put on a brave face to avoid burdening parents further. So, because of this, and parents' preoccupation with their own pain, children's needs are often overlooked.

Death of a parent

The death of a parent is generally thought to be the most traumatic event that can happen to a child. Morgan (1985) suggests that, when a parent dies, a child is faced with three major tasks:

(1) The child must come to terms with the reality of the death itself.
(2) The child must adapt to the changes in the family which will result from the loss of a parent.
(3) The child must learn to cope with the permanent absence of one parent.

Although guilt is probably an inevitable reaction to death for all ages it can be particularly devastating to a child. Young children may believe that bad things happen because they have been naughty, so they may blame themselves for their parent's death. Children may react by regressing to an earlier stage of development or may attempt to deny the reality of the death by carrying on as normal and apparently being unaffected by it. But then children are likely to experience physical symptoms such as loss of appetite or sleep problems.

Children sometimes exhibit hostile reactions to their dead parent and other people apparently because they feel they have been unjustly deserted by the deceased. Alternatively they may idealize the deceased as a means of avoiding the negative feelings they may have. Identifying with parents who have died by perhaps taking on some of their interests is seen as a constructive reaction. Whereas trying to take their place, perhaps even developing some of the symptoms which appeared during the illness, is considered to be potentially harmful and should be discouraged.

The way in which children react to the death of a parent will be influenced by three factors (Morgan, 1985). One important factor is the age of the child, as discussed later in this section. For example, very young children and preadolescents may be the most vulnerable – very young children because they are still dealing with the issue of separation from their parents and preadolescents because it is an important time for the development of sexual identity.

Another important factor is their relationship to the parent who has died. For young children the loss of the mother may have a bigger impact on them, particularly in traditional families where mothers spend considerably more time than fathers with the children. However, for boys who have reached school age the death of their father may be more significant because of the loss of a male figure to identify with and to help in disciplining them. For example, it has been found that higher rates of delinquency are recorded for boys who have lost their fathers than those who have had their mothers die. Also, when children are particularly close to one or other parent, as often happens, the loss of this parent will be more traumatic for them. In fact, in situations where children have a particularly strained relationship with one parent, the death of this parent can be accompanied by an improvement in their mental health.

Finally, a further factor in determining children's reactions to losing a parent is the extent to which previous losses and separations in their lives have been resolved. Children who are still coping with the death of someone close to them, such as a grandparent, may be particularly badly affected by the loss of a parent.

Morgan (1985) suggests that there are some common signs, which teachers should look for at school, that are indicative of children struggling to cope with the loss of a parent. These include: unsociability; despondency; forgetfulness; inattention; and a 'couldn't care less' attitude.

Death of a sibling

It is widely acknowledged that the death of a child is the most profound loss anyone can suffer and that parental grief is typically intense, debilitating and long-lasting. Romanoff (1993) has suggested that six elements contribute to the severity of the loss:

(1)   Children carry with them many of parents' hopes and wishes for the future so that when a child dies it is as if a part of the parent dies too.

(2)   Particularly when an only child dies, loss of the parenting role can for many parents challenge their accepted meaning or purpose in life.

(3)   Many parents have intense feelings of guilt about not preventing their child's death, no matter how irrational this may be. Also, because parents are struggling to cope with their own grief they often find it difficult to adequately care for their surviving children and also feel guilty about this.

(4)   Because the death of a child runs against the natural order of events it challenges parents' fundamental assumptions about the universe and can leave them feeling vulnerable and afraid for the safety of other family members.

(5)   Although parents tend to mourn their children as they existed at the time of death they also mourn for their lost opportunities to experience developmental stages as the child's surviving peers reach them.

(6)   Since childhood death is nowadays an infrequent event there is often a lack of other bereaved parents to offer shared understanding and support. This is particularly important since the other sources of support typically used by parents, such as their spouse, friends and relatives, may be emotionally unavailable to them due to coping with their own grieving for the child.

Romanoff suggests that counselling can help parents in several ways. It can help to normalize parental experiences by educating them about what to expect. It can help parents to search for meaning in the death of their child, something which is very difficult for parents to achieve by themselves. Counselling can also help parents to develop a redefined purpose in life without the child by, for example, encouraging them in altruistic actions such as participating in support groups or starting a memorial fund. Finally, counselling can help parents find ways to continue their relationships with children who have died through inner representations while reinvesting their energy in other relationships so that their lives can continue. For example, planting a tree or doing charitable work in the child's name or organizing a memorial service are ways in which parents can transform their relationship with their child who has died.

However, as noted earlier, very few parents avail themselves of counselling, which means that most parents are likely to be struggling to cope with their own grief for months or even years and therefore will be unable to provide sufficient help to their remaining children in coping with their reactions to the bereavement for possibly a substantial period of time. Morgan (1985) suggests that, when their own grief prevents parents from maintaining healthy parental relationships, surviving children are placed at risk of developing psychological problems. For example, younger children can react to the death of an older sibling by regressing to babyish behaviour in an attempt to prevent themselves growing to an age when death could occur. Alternatively, older children may become preoccupied with their own futures, anxious about whether they too will soon die.

Aware of their parents' grief, some children attempt to take the place of their dead sibling, perhaps by acting like them, even when this behaviour is not appropriate for their age. Children can experience considerable guilt, either about things done to, or not done for, dead siblings when they were alive, or about enjoying the feeling of having parents to themselves. If not recognized and dealt with during childhood these guilt feelings can lead to depression which can carry on into adult life and in extreme cases become a precursor to suicide (Morgan, 1985). Another possible problem occurs when parents displace their negative emotions on to siblings. As parents attempt to adapt to their loss, the anger and other intense emotions they experience may be displaced on to the surviving children who then sense their parents' hostility and feel that they are being punished for the death of their sibling.

Death of other significant people

It is often overlooked that the death of other family members such as grandparents, cousins, aunts or uncles can have a significant impact on children. This is especially so when there has been a particularly close relationship with the deceased. Also, the death of friends, classmates or teachers can be quite traumatic for children, as suggested in the case described above.

Incidents which involve the death of several schoolchildren, usually due to road accidents, tend to have a high profile because they are widely reported in the media. They actually happen quite infrequently but their impact when they do occur can be devastating to the families involved and to the children's schoolfriends. The impact is of course greatest on those children who survived the accident who commonly experience such reactions as depression, sleep disturbances, bedwetting, stomach problems, concentration difficulties and fear of hospitals, of being hurt or of dying (Morgan, 1985).

Unfortunately, the typical parental approach to children who have been affected by such an incident is to try to get them to forget the experience as quickly as possible. Parents not only avoid talking about it but also try to prevent children from discussing it with other people. Their reason for doing this appears to be a fear that children will become even more upset if they talk about it. Whereas, by not discussing it openly parents are adding to their children's trauma by indirectly suggesting that it is too frightening to deal with. In fact, parents are generally unaware that their unwillingness to discuss such things openly may have more to do with their anxiety about coping with their own reactions than about protecting their children.

The teacher's role

It is clear from the above discussion that a death in the family produces a situation for which parents need a great deal of help. Also, that the death of others with whom children have developed close relationships, such as friends, classmates and teachers, can be traumatic for children. Teachers are in the ideal position to provide help in coping with bereavement, both directly to the children concerned and indirectly through their parents (Thornton and Krajewski, 1993):

(1) Teachers have a knowledge of child development and are therefore aware of the different levels of understanding of death which children have at different ages.

(2) Teachers are also experienced observers of children's behaviour and since they see children five days a week are in an excellent position to notice any behavioural changes which may indicate difficulties they are having in coping with a bereavement.

(3) Teachers have access to information on death and grieving either through Personal and Social Education curriculum

material in their schools or through sources like those referenced in this section.

(4) Teachers will know of, or can find out about, the professional and voluntary help for the bereaved which is available in the local community.

(5) Teachers provide a vital link between school and home. They can work closely with parents to ensure that children's needs are met.

However, although teachers are well placed to help children and their parents cope with bereavement this frequently does not happen because death education has such a low profile in most schools. There has been a lack of training on the topic, and so most teachers simply do not know enough about the grieving process and how to help children cope with it. Therefore, the following sections provide a summary of the knowledge teachers need to have in order to help children directly or to be able to provide guidance to parents so they can help their children to cope with bereavement.

What parents and teachers both need in order to be able to help children cope with bereavement is information about how children of different ages understand and react to death. They also need guidelines for helping children to adjust to their loss.

Children's understanding of death

Children's understanding of death progresses from a complete lack of awareness through several phases of increased comprehension until an adult view is attained (Morgan, 1985). From birth to approximately 2 years of age children are considered to have no concept of death as such. They may experience grief in consequence of separation from people they have developed close relationships with but have no realization of the finality of death.

Three- to 5-year-olds tend to view death as being similar to sleep. They do not see it as a permanent state, nor do they understand that all living things must eventually die.

Between the ages of 5 and 9 years children come to realize the finality of death but are still not aware that it is universal. This usually happens from about 9 years of age when children may become upset at the idea of death in general and in particular about the possibility of their parents dying.

From 9 to 12 years children become aware of the finality, inevitability and universality of death and because of this often experience some anxiety associated with such thoughts.

Teenagers tend to become defiant of death, almost daring death to occur by playing games such as 'chicken', in which they run across the road in front of cars.

Grief in children

Some writers consider that children go through similar stages of grief to adults and therefore believe that their reactions are illustrated by the model of adaptation to loss which is described in Chapter 3. Other writers think that children's grieving is different, as suggested by the three-phase model proposed by Morgan (1985). The first phase is one of protest, when the child refuses to accept that the person is dead and, for some children, this involves angry attempts to get them back. In the second phase children experience hurt, despair and disorganization as they begin to accept the fact that the person has really gone. The third phase is one in which hope develops as children begin to reorganize their lives without the deceased.

Worden (1991) suggests that there are several key points which people working with children who have been bereaved need to be aware of:

- Experiencing the death of someone close is traumatic for children but need not lead to serious difficulties if appropriate help is given.
- How children mourn is determined by their levels of both cognitive and emotional development.
- Children aged 5 to 7 years are a particularly vulnerable group since their cognitive development is such that they are beginning to understand the finality of death but they do not have the personal and social skills to be able to cope with the situation.
- Mourning a childhood loss can be re-triggered at various points during adult life such as when the child gets married or reaches the same age as the parent who died.
- It is important for teachers and other professionals who work with children who have been bereaved to develop preventive approaches rather than waiting for problems to occur. In order to do this teachers need to understand the tasks involved in the process of mourning and to be familiar with the principles of grief counselling.

Grief counselling

Counselling must help the bereaved child to address the four tasks of mourning (Worden, 1991). These are:

- to accept the reality of the loss
- to experience and work through the pain of grief
- to adjust to an environment in which the deceased is missing
- to withdraw emotional energy from the deceased and transfer it to other relationships.

According to Worden (1991) there are ten major principles and procedures of grief counselling. The application of these principles to children who have suffered a bereavement is discussed below:

(1) *Helping the child actualize the loss.* The first task of grieving is to fully accept that the loss has occurred – that the person is dead and will not return. This can be facilitated by encouraging children to talk about the person who has died and how the death happened. Family members and friends typically discourage children from talking about such things either to spare their own pain or in the wrongly held belief that it is not helpful to dwell on the loss. However, like adults, children may need to talk about the death over and over again to someone who has the patience to listen. It may also be useful to suggest that children visit the grave of the deceased, or the place where their ashes have been scattered, and then encourage them to talk about their reactions.

(2) *Helping the child to identify and express feelings.* Helping children to become aware of and express their feelings about their loss is the most important task of grief counselling. For younger children drawing can be used both to identify hidden feelings and as a trigger for getting them to talk about how they feel (Allan, 1988). For older children getting them to write about the deceased can have a similar effect (Allan and Bertoia, 1992).

According to Worden (1991) the most problematic feelings experienced by people who have been bereaved are anger, guilt, sadness, anxiety and helplessness. It is difficult for adults, let alone children, to realize that they feel anger towards the deceased. So this anger is generally projected on to other members of the family or doctors or other children or even teachers. Sometimes the anger is turned inward and experienced as depression or guilt. Older children may feel guilty about how they behaved towards the deceased. Younger children may feel guilty because they believe that they were in some way responsible for the death.

Sadness is a natural reaction to a major loss but the expression of sadness is often problematic. This is because it is best expressed through crying which in some societies is discouraged since it is regarded as a sign of weakness. In other societies, such as among New Zealand Maoris and Jewish people, public crying is encouraged at funerals, which enables a healthy expression of sadness.

The anxiety experienced by bereaved children is partly related to their feelings of helplessness, of not being able to cope without the deceased parent or sibling. The anxiety also stems from children's increased awareness of the vulnerability of other family members and themselves to death.

(3)   *Helping the child to live life without the deceased.* As well as coping with their grief, bereaved children also need to be able to deal with the practical difficulties which result from their loss. A child who has lost a parent or an older sibling will probably be expected to take on more responsibility around the home. A child who has lost a close friend will need to seek out other friendships. Teachers helping children to adjust to these practical difficulties need to use a problem-solving approach to counselling such as that described in Chapter 5.

(4)   *Helping the child to reinvest emotional energy.* Children need to be helped to find ways of maintaining the memory of the person who has died while reinvesting their energy in other relationships so that their lives can continue. For example, they can be encouraged to keep a journal of their thoughts about the deceased to help them see that by developing new relationships they are not forgetting the person who has died.

(5)   *Providing time to grieve.* There is an expectation in most Western societies that people should 'get over' a major loss in a few months. In more traditional societies such as the Maori and Jewish cultures, referred to above, it is recognized that this is not the case. Both of these cultures have a memorial ceremony one year after the death to mark the end of the official period of mourning. Most experts in grief counselling agree that it generally takes up to two years for a child or an adult to adjust to any major loss. Also, that this only applies if people are grieving during this time and not avoiding expressing their feelings in which case it may take much longer.

(6)   *Providing ongoing support.* Children will need continuing support for at least a year following the death, and probably longer. Certain times may be particularly difficult for them, such as birthdays, Christmas and the anniversary of the death. Bereavement support groups (discussed below) can be very helpful, so parents and children should be made aware of their existence in the local community.

(7)   *Interpreting normal behaviour.* Children can become frightened by their thoughts and feelings following the death of someone close. It is therefore helpful to be able to explain the grieving

process to them, including a discussion of typical reactions, in order to reassure them about the normality of what they are experiencing.

(8) *Allowing for individual differences.* It is also important to explain to children that the reactions triggered by grief will be different for each person. Their surviving siblings, parents and friends will all be grieving in different ways.

(9) *Examining defences and coping style.* Some of the ways in which children (and adults) cope with a bereavement are not healthy because they involve using defences to avoid experiencing the pain of grieving. For example, children who withdraw from contact with friends and family or refuse to talk about or look at photographs of the deceased are using defence mechanisms to avoid facing up to their grief and need help in order to develop more effective coping strategies.

(10) *Identifying pathology and referring.* The listening and counselling skills discussed in Chapter 5 are sufficient for teachers to be able to help the majority of children to cope with bereavement. However, these will not be sufficient for a minority of children who are experiencing severe difficulties coping with their loss and who will therefore need more intensive help. Also, some teachers will feel that they do not have the expertise, time or patience to counsel children who have been bereaved. It is important to recognize one's limitations and be prepared to suggest to the headteacher or to parents that professional counselling is required.

Guidelines for working with children

Guidelines for teachers in working with bereaved children individually, or for class teaching about grief and bereavement, perhaps as part of the school's Personal and Social Development programme, are clear from the above discussion. The key points include:

- encouraging children to express feelings
- discussing death in terms that children can understand
- giving children information about death and grief suitable for their developmental level
- suggesting appropriate ways in which children can remember the deceased
- encouraging the adoption of healthy and effective coping strategies.

The ways in which teachers react to and deal with death is vitally important since they act as models for their pupils. The impact on pupils of a teacher's approach to death was illustrated by a recent letter written by a mother whose 17-year-old son had drowned (Mulder, 1994). In the letter, this bereaved mother recounted how the schools which her surviving children attended had both instructed the other pupils not to mention the death to them in case it upset them. However, her 10-year-old daughter's teacher had recently been bereaved herself and ignored this advice. She told the daughter's classmates that they should say how sorry they were about her loss and allow her to talk about her brother if and when she wanted to. On the other hand, pupils at the school which the writer's 14-year-old son attended followed the instructions and did not mention his brother's death. The result was that, while her daughter felt surrounded by love and concern, her son was confused and hurt by the apparent lack of concern which his school friends showed and was also deprived of the support which his sister had found so valuable.

Guidelines for working with parents

In addition to what teachers of bereaved children do at school they can be an invaluable support and resource for parents. Guidelines for teachers in working with parents of children who have been bereaved are outlined below.

Two-way communication Keeping open channels of communication between school and home by such means as phone contacts, meetings and notes sent home (as discussed in Chapter 6) is the most important thing teachers can do to help parents. In this way concerns which either teachers or parents have about how children are coping can be shared and strategies for helping children can be agreed.

Providing guidance Teachers can provide invaluable guidance to parents based on their knowledge of child development and of the effects of bereavement on children. Their knowledge of the children concerned and the working relationship they have established with the parents place them in an excellent position to provide this guidance. Teachers can recommend to parents books about how to help children cope with their grief such as that by Dyregrov (1991). They can also recommend books written for parents who have lost a child such as the powerful and moving book by Schiff (1977) and that by Rando (1988). In addition, they can suggest to parents books on death for surviving siblings to read (see Ordal, 1984).

Providing counselling Teachers can provide supportive counselling to parents in order to help them cope with the effects of the loss on themselves and other family members. Mainly, what parents need is someone who can listen in order to help them clarify their thoughts and feelings and help them to decide what to do about the various problems they face. The basic listening and counselling skills which teachers need in order to help parents in this way are discussed in Chapter 5. Most teachers do not have the time or skills to take on intensive or long-term counselling of parents, but even a brief session in which parents are encouraged to open up and enabled to see the value of counselling can make them more likely to agree to being referred to sources of more specialized counselling and support.

Referring parents to other sources of counselling and support Teachers can help by making parents aware of the counselling services available in their community, particularly any which offer specialized help for people who have been bereaved. A very important source of support for parents and other members of families who have suffered a death are the bereavement groups which are now available in most communities. Such groups can help participants: gain hope; feel less isolated; develop feelings of fellowship; get information on other sources of help; and, develop support networks (Hopmeyer and Werk, 1993). Often the most valuable things which people report gaining from participating in these groups are a feeling of not being alone in their grief and the opportunity to share thoughts and feelings with others who can understand. Some groups are peer-led, others are co-led by a professional and a peer facilitator. They can be ongoing and open to new participants at any time or alternatively involve a predetermined number of meetings in which case they may be closed to new participants once they have begun. Whatever the organization, such groups can be an important source of support for the bereaved.

CHILDREN COPING WITH THEIR PARENTS' SEPARATION OR DIVORCE

Figures from the 1991 census show that, in Britain, one in three marriages ends in divorce. Therefore, before they reach the age of 16, one in five children will experience the divorce of their parents, while an unknown number are affected by parental separation (Cox and Desforges, 1987). It has been estimated that around two-thirds of children will exhibit noticeable changes in behaviour at school following parental separation. The types of behaviour which are associated with parental separation and divorce include:

- restlessness
- day-dreaming
- withdrawal
- concentration problems
- aggressiveness
- acting out
- depression
- regression to an earlier stage of development
- loss of self-confidence
- oversensitivity to criticism
- peer relationship difficulties
- deterioration in academic achievement
- delinquency.

Children who experience the separation or divorce of their parents are therefore at risk of developing emotional and behavioural difficulties (Hodges, 1991). The likelihood that such difficulties will result depends partly on the extent to which their special needs are met within the school. In order for teachers to provide for the special needs of these children they need to know about the family difficulties which they are likely to experience and about the reactions to parental separation common to children of different ages. These aspects are discussed below.

Effects of separation and divorce on family members

Family disruption is often a serious problem in the first year after a separation. Parents tend to be so involved with their own feelings and concerns in adjusting to their new situation that they overlook the needs of their children. Discipline in the home can be inconsistent and parents may not notice the pain which children are experiencing. So at the very time when children need most support their parents are least able to provide it because they are overwhelmed by their own problems. Studies of families where there has been a divorce, conducted in the USA (Morgan, 1985), have shown that at least one member of each family has exhibited disruptive behaviour or serious distress. In most cases the most seriously affected family members are the children. However, it must not be forgotten that parental divorce has an impact on all family members, including the extended family, especially grandparents, who face the possibility of being denied access to their grandchildren (Myers and Perrin, 1993).

Children's ability to cope with parental separation

A variety of factors contribute to a child's ability to cope with parental separation (Morgan, 1985). These are outlined below.

Age and gender of the child In general, the older the child at the time of divorce the less detrimental effects there will be. However, there are differences in the ways children of different ages react to parental separation and these are discussed in the following section. Boys are generally considered to have more problems than girls in adjusting to divorce because typically it is the father who leaves the family home, depriving boys of a male figure with whom to identify.

Maturity of the child How well children cope will depend on their emotional maturity and whether there are any other complicating issues in the child's life. For example, adopted children whose parents are divorcing tend to have greater difficulties coping with the situation than other children.

Financial situation of the parents Often when one parent leaves the family home both parents face financial hardship. This may mean that custodial parents find it difficult to spare money for children to go on school trips or that non-custodial parents may not be able to afford to come to see children, or to take them out, as often as they would like.

Degree of discord before the divorce For families in which there has been considerable conflict, hostility and instability, separation and subsequent divorce of the parents may be accompanied by feelings of relief in the children. Divorce may be easier for children in this situation to accept than for those in families where parents have kept their disagreements away from the children.

Extent of conflict after the divorce When both parents co-operate in maintaining relationships with their children following separation it is much easier for children to adjust to the situation than when there is continual animosity between the parents. The most difficult situation for children to cope with is the one in which parents try to sour or break off the relationships between their children and the other parent. This situation almost inevitably leads to children experiencing emotional or behavioural difficulties.

Child's relationship with each parent When a child is particularly close to the parent who moves out of the family home the separation will be much more difficult for the child to adjust to than when the child is closer to the parent who remains in the home.

Child's relationship with siblings Children who have siblings typically find it easier to cope with divorce than only children since parental separation usually leads to siblings developing closer relationships with each other.

Child's own ability to cope with stress Children will cope with the stress associated with parental separation in their own idiosyncratic ways. Exactly how they react will be influenced by their past experiences of coping with traumatic events.

Availability of emotional support A major factor in determining how well children will cope with the divorce of their parents is the availability of people to talk to about their concerns and feelings. As suggested above, they may receive some support from their siblings but other family members are likely to be too concerned with their own feelings to be able to help. This emphasizes the importance of children gaining support from people outside the family. Teachers are therefore key sources of support since they typically know children better than any adult outside their families and can be confidential and objective in providing help.

Effects on children at different ages

Pre-school age children have difficulty fully understanding the situation and tend to react in one of two ways. They either attempt to deny the reality of the separation by pretending that nothing has changed or they become very upset and regress to more immature behaviour with perhaps loss of independence in dressing, feeding or toileting. Pre-school children often fear the loss of the other parent when one has left the family home, so they may cling more closely to the remaining parent and tend to get very upset at routine separations (Cox and Desforges, 1987).

Children of primary school age tend to find it particularly difficult to adjust to parental separation since they understand enough about the situation to make denial a less useful option than with younger children but at the same time they have not developed the coping strategies which older children typically use (Morgan, 1985). Common problems at this age are therefore associated with the feelings of guilt or anxiety which children may experience. They may feel guilty believing that in some way they have caused the separation, or they may become anxious about the possibility of the other parent leaving them. Many younger primary school age children experience feelings of intense sadness or depression which they find very difficult to understand. They can be highly emotional with aggressive behaviour alternating wildly with episodes of crying (Hodges, 1991).

Children of secondary school age tend to experience either anger or depression. Their academic work may be seriously affected or they may participate in delinquent acts (Morgan, 1985). They often experience embarrassment about the family breakup and try to keep it a secret from their friends. They are much less likely than younger children to use denial or to regress in their behaviour. They have the ability to express their opinions and feelings including their anger towards the parent they blame for the separation. Conflicts between both the parents and their teenage children may be intensified by the divorce.

What teachers can do to help

Teachers are in an excellent position to help children cope with effects of divorce and to provide guidance to parents. Teachers are knowledgeable about child development and are skilled in the observation and analysis of children's behaviour. They are therefore able to identify changes in children's behaviour which are indicative of their difficulties in adjusting to parental separation or divorce. Teachers are also in regular contact with children and have the opportunity to develop sufficient rapport for them to feel comfortable enough to open up and talk about the things that are bothering them. In addition, when teachers develop two-way communication with parents (as discussed in Chapter 6) they are in an ideal position to provide guidance to parents and to collaborate with them in dealing with children's difficulties.

Many children, whose parents have separated or divorced, report that they would have liked someone at the school to encourage them to talk about their feelings and reactions to their situation and to suggest relevant books for them to read (Morgan, 1985). A range of specific strategies which teachers can employ to help children cope with the separation of their parents have been suggested by Cox and Desforges (1987). These are discussed below.

Developing a school policy Teachers need to acquaint themselves with the school policy for dealing with the separation or divorce of pupils attending the school. They need to know what is expected of teachers and of parents in the event of a separation. A school's expectations of parents in this situation should be written in the handbook which parents receive when their child enters the school. The statement need simply say that the school should be informed about any disruptions in home circumstances, including parental separation, which may affect a child's behaviour or progress at school.

Organizing support at school For children who are experiencing disruption and unhappiness at home the school can provide a haven of calm and security which itself is very therapeutic. In addition, having a well organized system of pastoral care is very important so that pupils have the opportunity to develop a good rapport with their class teacher or form tutor, and head of year or head of house. Teachers acting in their pastoral capacity can thereby provide children extra attention and support in order to help them cope with their parents' separation. Other members of the school staff, such as teacher aides and dinner ladies, can also provide such help since pupils with difficulties often form a rapport with them. Teachers can also ensure that the Personal and Social Education curriculum used in the school includes sessions on coping with parental separation and divorce. Alternatively, the topic can be made the subject of class discussions held during form tutor periods, using a developmental strategy such as that proposed by Allan and Nairne (1984) which uses an approach similar to that of the counselling model presented in Chapter 5.

Keeping records It is helpful for teachers to keep records of the family circumstances of the pupils for whom they are responsible. Teachers need to have the names and addresses of both natural parents and any step-parents. They need to record when the separations and divorces have occurred and to have a record of the custody and access arrangements for each child whose parents have divorced. For example, is custody shared or does the child live mainly with one parent and see the other only at weekends? Teachers also need to record any legal restrictions placed on contacts between children and one or other of their parents. In addition, it is useful to keep a record of the problems which children have experienced at school since the separation. These records need to be continually updated and can eventually be made available to subsequent teachers.

Providing counselling Teachers are in an excellent position to provide supportive counselling both to parents who have separated and to their children. Pupils are more likely to open up and talk about their problems with teachers or other school staff with whom they have developed a good rapport than with outside specialists such as educational psychologists or education welfare officers. The same applies to parents. They are much more likely to talk about their concerns to their children's teacher than to a professional counsellor. This is especially so when the teacher has established two-way communication with parents, as discussed in Chapter 6.

In order to provide supportive counselling to pupils and parents, teachers need to develop the listening and counselling skills discussed in Chapter 5. The model of counselling presented in Chapter 5 is one which is suitable for dealing with the vast majority of problems likely to be of concern to parents and children. However, the model emphasizes the importance of knowing when to refer on parents or pupils for more specialist help. For example, while teachers may be happy to counsel parents about difficulties their children are having it would be more appropriate to refer parents who want to discuss their own relationship problems to a specialist agency such as Relate.

Involving both parents When teachers continue to involve both parents following a separation or divorce it sends an important message to the children and their parents. This message is that children need both parents to be interested in their education and welfare despite the fact that they are now living apart. It is therefore important for teachers to send letters of invitation and copies of school reports to each of the parents. Divorced parents should be given the opportunity to decide whether they will attend parents' evenings together or separately. If they are able to attend together then the school can provide a neutral setting for parents to discuss their children's education. If necessary, teachers can act as child advocates, mediating on any conflict between parents.

Providing practical help Teachers can provide help to divorced parents whose children live with them on a number of practical matters. Since many families experience financial difficulties following a separation or divorce teachers can check whether children are eligible for free school meals. Receiving free school meals not only eases the financial burden on parents but also communicates to other members of staff that parents may find it difficult to provide money for school trips and the like. At times of family disruption children may not be able to find a calm place to do their homework so the provision of a homework centre at the school can be a tremendous help. Practical considerations, such as providing a safe place for pupils to leave bags packed ready for weekend access visits, can make life easier for children and also reinforce the acceptability of their situation.

Providing relevant reading material Teachers can help children adjust to their new situation by ensuring they have access to books which deal with separation and divorce such as those by Mitchell (1982) and Townsend (1982). Teachers can also suggest books, such as those by Burgoyne (1984) and Visher and Visher (1982), to parents which will help them to gain a better understanding of their children's needs following a separation.

SUMMARY AND CONCLUSIONS

This chapter has focused on how teachers can be of help to parents of children with four different types of special needs. Children with disabilities and medical conditions were considered first, followed by children who have been bereaved and finally children whose parents have separated or divorced.

The typical effects of childhood disability on families, mothers, fathers, siblings, grandparents and the marital relationship were briefly discussed. Then, several different ways in which teachers could help parents were proposed, including establishing two-way communication and considering the whole family's needs.

Children with chronic and life-threatening illnesses were considered next. The effects on these children and their families were discussed and what teachers can do to help was outlined, including the importance of liaison with health service personnel. This was followed by a discussion of the special needs of children affected by a bereavement. Children's difficulties in coping with the death of a parent, a sibling or another person with whom they had a close relationship were considered. This section then focused on children's understanding of death at different ages and the principles of grief counselling applied to children. Then, guidelines for teachers in working with bereaved children and their parents were outlined.

Finally, the special needs of children whose parents have separated or divorced were discussed. The effects of parental separation on families was considered, specifically the factors associated with a child's ability to adjust to the new situation and the effects on children of different ages. Strategies which teachers can use to help the parents of these children were outlined, including developing a school policy and providing counselling.

In conclusion, it is clear that, in addition to providing appropriately for these children's special needs at school, teachers can be of invaluable assistance to their parents. In order to work effectively with parents, teachers need to have high levels of interpersonal communication skills. These skills are considered in the following chapter.

5

Interpersonal skills for working with parents

INTRODUCTION

While in Bangalore a few years ago, I was told a story that I have heard many times before but which bears retelling because its message is so important. A parent who has a daughter who is mentally handicapped told me how a young mother whose child had just been diagnosed with a disability had come to him for help. They had talked for over two hours but my friend felt frustrated because he was not able to provide any practical help for the mother. He felt particularly inadequate because in India, as in many other traditional cultures, people who seek help expect to be given specific advice to follow. Therefore, it was much to his surprise when, two weeks later, the young mother called in to see my friend to thank him for all the help he had given her when they last met! He was surprised because all he had done had been to listen with understanding to what his fellow parent had to say.

Many teachers will have heard similar stories in which people have found out by chance just how helpful it is to have someone *really listen* when the other person has a concern they need to talk over. Teachers cannot fail to be aware of the importance of listening in education since listening skills are enshrined in one of the attainment targets in the English National Curriculum. How is it then, that when parents of children with special needs are asked how they would like professionals to change, the most common response is that they would like professionals to listen more? Somehow our knowledge of the importance of listening doesn't get translated into practice.

In order to work effectively with parents, teachers need to have good interpersonal communication skills. While teachers typically have excellent skills in the areas of verbal presentation, explanation and information-giving, they generally have less well developed skills in the areas of listening, counselling and assertiveness (Seligman, 1979; Turnbull and Turnbull, 1986). These three skill areas are particularly important for working with parents and therefore are the focus of this chapter.

Probably the most important of the three sets of skills are the ones needed for effective listening. These include the skills of attentiveness, passive listening, paraphrasing and active listening. Other interpersonal skills, which are needed for communicating with parents and for collaborating with colleagues, are assertion skills. These include techniques for making and refusing requests, giving constructive feedback, handling criticism and problem-solving.

Also useful are basic counselling skills, particularly if set within a problem-solving model of counselling which involves listening and assertion skills. To use such a model teachers must first of all listen to what parents have to say, in order to help them clarify their concerns or ideas. Parents should then be helped to gain a clear understanding of the problem situation which they face or goal which they have. Finally, teachers should help parents decide what, if anything, they want to do about their concern or idea. That is, what action they wish to take. Possessing the skills required to implement this simple model of counselling will contribute enormously to the ability of teachers to establish a productive working relationship with parents. A three-stage problem-solving counselling model is presented later in this chapter, following the discussion of listening and assertion skills.

LISTENING SKILLS

A discussion of the skills required for effective listening to take place is presented below. The major components of listening are: attentiveness; passive listening; paraphrasing; and active listening (Bolton, 1979; Brammer, 1988).

Attentiveness

Effective listening requires a high level of attentiveness. This involves focusing one's physical attention on the person being listened to and includes several components.

Eye contact The importance for the listener of maintaining good eye contact cannot be overemphasized. While parents are talking they may not look directly at the teacher for most of the time but will occasionally look across to check that he or she is listening. Therefore, it is important to maintain eye contact throughout the interview. In situations where someone feels uncomfortable with direct eye contact it is usually satisfactory for the listener to look at the speaker's mouth or the tip of their nose instead. Speakers generally cannot tell the difference.

Facing squarely To communicate attentiveness it is important for the listener to face the other person squarely or at a slight angle. Turning one's body away from another person suggests that you are not totally with them.

Leaning forward Leaning slightly forward, towards the person being listened to, communicates attentiveness. Alternatively, leaning backwards gives the impression that you are not listening.

Open posture Having one's legs crossed, or even worse, one's arms crossed when one is listening gives the impression of a lack of openness, as if a barrier is being placed between the listener and the person talking. Attentiveness is best communicated by the adoption of an open posture with both arms and legs uncrossed. However, many women feel most comfortable sitting with their legs crossed at the knees and would not be able to remain as relaxed with their legs uncrossed. This does not significantly reduce their attentiveness.

Remaining relaxed It is essential to be relaxed while adopting an attentive posture since if the posture adopted is not comfortable it is not possible to concentrate fully on what is being said. Therefore, it is important to take up an attentive posture in which one feels relaxed, even if this doesn't exactly follow the guidelines discussed above.

Appropriate body motion It is important to avoid distracting movements such as looking at the clock, fiddling with a pen, or constantly changing position. In addition, it is important to move appropriately in response to the speaker since a listener who sits perfectly still can be quite unnerving and may not communicate attentiveness.

Non-distracting environment It is not easy to listen attentively in an environment in which there are distractions. The room used should be as quiet as possible and the door should be kept closed. Telephone calls should be put on hold and a 'meeting in progress' sign hung on the door. Within the room the chairs used should be comfortable and there should be no physical barrier, such as a desk, between teacher and parent.

Distance There needs to be a suitable distance between speaker and listener. If the distance is too great or too small then the speaker will feel uncomfortable and this will impede the communication. A distance of about three feet is usually recommended but this can vary between cultures so it is best to always look for signs of discomfort or anxiety in the listener and adjust the distance accordingly.

Passive listening

Passive listening involves using a high level of attentiveness combined with other skills. These are: invitations to talk; non-verbal grunts; open questions; attentive silence; avoiding communication blocks; and minimizing self-listening.

Invitations to talk Before the teacher can begin to listen, parents need to be invited to talk about their concern or idea. For example, 'How can I help you?' or 'You seem upset. Would you like to talk about it?' The specific wording of the invitation needs to be tailored to the situation and people involved.

Non-verbal grunts There are various sounds or short words which are often known as 'non-verbal grunts', because they let the speaker know that you are with them without interrupting the flow. For example, 'Go on', 'Right', 'Huh Huh', 'Mm Mm'. It is particularly important to use these while listening to someone on the telephone because the speaker cannot gauge the listener's attentiveness through the usual visual clues.

Open questions Open questions are used for clarification or to encourage the speaker to continue. For example, 'How do you mean?' or 'What happened then?' Closed questions, which usually require a very brief response such as 'yes' or 'no' and allow the listener to set the agenda, are avoided. This can be very hard for teachers to do since they typically spend much of their time in classrooms asking closed questions and it is difficult to change this strategy quickly.

Attentive silence Teachers should pause for a few seconds after each thing they say to give parents the opportunity to say more or to remain silent. During silences, parents are often clarifying their thoughts and feelings. Therefore, using attentive silence is a very effective way of encouraging people to open up and continue exploring their concerns or ideas.

Avoiding communication blocks Certain types of comment tend to act as blocks to the communication process and therefore must be avoided (Gordon, 1970). When used they stop parents from exploring their concerns and ideas. Common examples are: *criticism*, *sarcasm*, *advice giving*, or *reassurance*, such as saying 'Don't worry, it will work out all right'.

Another type of block which is particularly annoying to parents is *denial* or *false acknowledgement of feelings*, such as suggesting that parents should 'Look on the bright side' or telling them 'I know exactly how you feel'.

Other common blocks involve *diverting* parents from the topic, either directly or by the use of *excessive questioning* or by *excessive self-disclosure* when people go on about themselves or others they have known who have had similar problems. Further blocks involve *moralizing*, *ordering* or *threatening*, that is, telling parents what they ought or must do. Finally, there are the blocks in which *diagnosis* or *labelling* is used. For example, telling someone that they are 'a worrier'. All the blocks tend to stifle the exploration of concerns or ideas and therefore should be avoided.

Avoiding self-listening Self-listening occurs when people drift off into their own thoughts rather than listening to what the other person is saying. When a teacher is listening to a parent and begins to self-listen there is a likelihood that important aspects of what is said will be missed. The teacher may then become confused and will be unable to respond effectively to the parent, who will therefore become aware of the inadequacy of the listening and tend to clam up. This is why it is very important that when teachers are listening to parents they are able to reduce self-listening to a minimum. The best way of minimizing self-listening is to use the listening techniques discussed below.

Paraphrasing

Paraphrasing is a skill which most people already use to some extent. When someone has told us something important and we want to be sure that we have understood correctly, we feed back the main points of the message to the person for his or her confirmation. This is a crude form of paraphrasing which is similar to that used by competent listeners.

An effective paraphrase has four components.

(1) The paraphrase feeds back only the key points of the speaker's message.

(2) Paraphrasing is concerned with the factual content of the speaker's message, not with feelings.

(3)   An effective paraphrase is short and to the point. It is a summary of the speaker's key message, not a summary of everything said.
(4)   A paraphrase is stated in the listener's own words but in language which is familiar to the speaker.

Paraphrases are used when there are natural breaks in the inter-action, such as when the speaker pauses and looks at the listener or when the speaker inflects his or her voice at the end of a sentence, clearly wanting some response from the listener. At this point the listener feeds back the essence of the speaker's message and then waits for a response. When the paraphrase hits the mark the speaker typically indicates that this is the case by saying 'That's it' or 'Right' or 'Yes' or by some non-verbal means such as nodding his or her head.

If the paraphrase is not accurate, or only partly accurate, then the response will not be so positive and in most cases the speaker will correct the listener. In so doing the speaker will also be clarifying for himself or herself exactly what is meant, so the paraphrase will still have been of value.

Active listening

Active listening is generally understood to involve trying to under-stand what the person is feeling and what the key message is in what they are saying, then putting this understanding into your own words and feeding it back to the person (Gordon, 1970). Thus, active listening involves the listener being actively engaged in clarifying the thoughts and feelings of the person they are with. It builds on attentiveness, passive listening and also paraphrasing, in that the main aspects of what is being communicated are reflected back to the person. This is done to provide a kind of 'sounding-board' to facilitate exploration and clarification of the person's concerns, ideas and feelings.

Gordon (1970) suggested that certain attitudes are essential pre-requisites to active listening. These are that the listener must:

- really want to hear what the other person has to say
- sincerely want to help the other person with his or her concern
- be able to respect the other person's feelings or values even though they conflict with his or her own
- have faith in the other person's ability to work through and solve his or her own problems
- realize that feelings are transitory and not be afraid when people express strong feelings such as anger or sadness

- accept that other people may have very different opinions, attitudes and values to themselves.

The process of active listening involves reflecting both thoughts and feelings back to the speaker. The speaker's key feeling is fed back along with the apparent reason for the feeling. When teachers are learning how to use active listening it is useful to have a set formula to follow. The formula 'You *feel* . . . *because* . . .' is typically used. For example: 'You *feel* frustrated *because* you haven't finished the job', and 'You *feel* delighted *because* she has done so well'.

When teachers gain confidence in their use of active listening the formula is no longer needed and thoughts and feelings can be reflected back in a more natural way. For example: 'You *are* angry *about* the way you were treated', 'You're sad *that* it has come to an end', 'You *were* pleased *with* the result', and 'You *were* annoyed *by* her manner'.

However, active listening involves much more than simply using this formula. It requires the listener to set aside his or her own perspective in order to understand what the other person is experiencing. It therefore involves being aware of how things are said, the expressions and gestures used and, most importantly, of hearing what is not said but which lies behind what is said. The real art in active listening is in feeding this awareness back to the person accurately and sensitively. This, of course, is very difficult, but the beauty of active listening is that you don't have to be completely right to be helpful. An active listening response which is a little off the mark typically gets the person who is talking to clarify his or her thoughts and feelings further. However, active listening responses which are way off the mark suggest to the speaker that the other person isn't listening and therefore can act as blocks to communication.

ASSERTION SKILLS

Assertiveness involves being able to stand up for one's own rights while respecting the rights of others; being able to communicate one's ideas, concerns and needs directly, persistently and diplomatically; being able to express both positive and negative feelings with openness and honesty; and being able to choose how to react to situations from a range of options.

Teachers need assertion skills both for working with parents and for collaborating with their colleagues. Teachers will have to deal with criticism or aggression from time to time and will need to make and refuse requests. They will also need to be able to give constructive feedback. Finally, they will need to be able to help people solve problems. The skills involved in these situations are outlined below and are discussed in more detail elsewhere (Hornby, 1994b; Bolton, 1979).

Basic elements of assertiveness

There are three aspects of assertiveness which apply in any situation. These are: physical assertiveness; vocal assertiveness; and assertion muscle levels.

Physical assertiveness Assertive body language is a key component of effective assertion. The components of physical assertiveness are similar to those of the attentiveness required for effective listening: an open posture, facing the other person squarely, standing or sitting erect or leaning slightly forward, maintaining good eye contact, not fidgeting or using superfluous gestures. What is different about assertiveness is that the facial expression should match the seriousness of the message and also that feet should be firmly planted on the floor, even when sitting.

Vocal assertiveness To optimize the effectiveness of the message the voice should be firm but calm. It is best to speak a little more slowly than usual but at a normal volume and to breathe deeply as this will help to ensure that there is enough breath to speak firmly and to maintain calmness.

Assertion muscle levels Whenever one is being assertive it is important to select the appropriate strength or 'muscle level' of the assertive response used. Usually, one should start at the lowest muscle level, or assertion strength, which is likely to achieve success. For example, 'I would appreciate it if you could . . .'. If this doesn't work the muscle level is increased and the request repeated. For example, 'It is important that you . . .'. Muscle levels are then progressively increased until a satisfactory response is obtained. For example, from 'It is essential that you . . .' to finally 'I demand that you . . .'.

At the same time that verbal muscle levels are being increased, physical and vocal assertiveness should also be gradually made more intense. That is, by using a more serious facial expression and a firmer tone of voice with each increase in muscle level.

Responding to criticism

Teachers will occasionally get criticism from their colleagues and sometimes from parents. Important factors involved in determining the impact of criticism are the intention of the person giving it and whether it comes with constructive suggestions for change. Holland and Ward (1990) have described a four-step approach which is useful in considering how to respond to criticism. The four steps of the model are outlined below.

Step 1: Listening to the criticism Listening skills are useful in clarifying the criticism. Open questions such as 'How do you mean?' or 'Can you be more specific?' are helpful in finding out exactly what the criticism is aimed at.

Step 2: Deciding on the truth Before responding to the criticism its validity should be considered. It may be completely true, partly true or completely untrue. One's assessment of the validity of the criticism will determine the response used in Step 3.

Step 3: Responding assertively If we consider the criticism to be completely true then it is best to agree with the criticizer, make a brief apology and assure them you will correct the situation. For example, 'I'm sorry about not consulting you on this matter. I'll make sure it doesn't happen again.'

If we consider the criticism is partly true then we should agree with the part considered to be valid, briefly apologize, and at the same time correct the part which is false. For example, 'Yes, I did make a mistake in that case and I regret that, but I don't accept that I'm making mistakes all the time these days. I make occasional errors like anyone else.'

If we consider the criticism to be completely false then we should clearly reject it, tell the other person exactly how the criticism makes us feel, ask for an explanation of their comments and make an affirmative statement about ourselves. For example, 'I don't agree that I was wrong in that case and am greatly offended by the suggestion. What grounds could you possibly have for making such a comment? I believe my relationships with pupils are excellent.'

Step 4: Letting go Decide to use what you have learned from the criticism and about the criticizer and move on. I know this is much easier said than done, but we must not let ourselves be deflected from our goals by what is, after all, just one person's opinion.

Dealing with aggression

Occasionally teachers have to deal with aggressive behaviour from parents or colleagues. Kroth (1985) has provided some guidelines for what teachers should do and should not do in this situation. *Teachers should not:*

- argue with a person who is behaving aggressively
- raise their voices or begin to shout
- become defensive and feel they have to defend their position
- attempt to minimize the concern which the other person is expressing
- take responsibility for problems which are not of their making
- make promises which they won't be able to fulfil.

All of these responses are ones which are commonly used by people confronted with aggression but they seldom work and are more likely to make the other person more aggressive. The following responses are far more likely to calm the other person down and lead to a constructive resolution of the situation. *Teachers should:*

- actively listen to the other person, reflecting back their thoughts and feelings in order to confirm that you are listening and to help you understand their perspective
- speak, softly, slowly and calmly
- ask for clarification of any complaints which are vague
- ask them what else is bothering them in order to exhaust their list of complaints
- make a list of their concerns, show them the list and ask if it's correct and complete
- use the techniques of problem-solving, discussed below, to work through their list of concerns in order to resolve the problems or conflicts, starting with the one of highest priority to the other person.

Refusing a request

Teachers will sometimes receive requests from parents or colleagues which they think they shouldn't agree to but feel unable to turn down. People have difficulty saying 'no' for several reasons but especially due to the fear that it will damage their relationship with the other person. The alternative to agreeing to requests you would rather turn down is to use acceptable ways of saying 'no', several of which are listed below.

The explained 'no' When you have a genuine reason for the refusal you can say 'no', explain why you are turning down the request, and give a brief apology. For example, 'No, I'm sorry, I can't make it because I'm already booked for that day'.

The postponed 'no' In this refusal you explain that you can't comply with the request at present but may be able to in the future. For example, 'No, I'm sorry, I'm not able to take that on today, but I may be able to help you with it in the future'.

The delayed 'no' In this technique you ask for time to think it over. This gives you the opportunity to carefully consider whether you want to comply with the request and to work out exactly how you will say 'no'. For example, 'I'm busy right now and I'd like to give it some thought. Can I get back to you tomorrow?'

The listening 'no' In this refusal active listening skills are used to let other people know that you understand the reason for their request. The listening response is combined with a brief apology and a firm refusal. For example, 'Yes, I understand your frustration about not being able to get the job done. I'm sorry, but I can't help you with it.'

The 'get back to me' 'no'. This involves explaining the difficulties you have in complying with the request. Then suggesting that the person try elsewhere and, if all else fails, come back to you and you'll see what you can do. For example, 'I'm busy for the next two weeks, so I suggest you try elsewhere. If you really get stuck I'll do my best to fit you in but I can't promise anything.'

The 'broken record' 'no' This is a form of refusal which is particularly useful for dealing with people who won't take 'no' for an answer. It involves making a brief statement of refusal to the other person, avoiding getting into discussion with them, and simply repeating the statement as many times as necessary (like a broken record) until the message gets across.

Making a request

Teachers sometimes need to request various things from their colleagues and occasionally need to make requests of parents. So, being able to make requests effectively is important, especially since many people find it difficult. Manthei (1981) has provided some useful guidelines for making requests:

- State your request directly – state your request firmly and clearly to the other person.
- Say exactly what you want – be specific and precise about your requirements.
- Focus on the positive – create an expectation of compliance.

- Answer only questions seeking clarification – don't allow yourself to be sidetracked.
- Allow the person time to think about it – suggest you'll get back to them tomorrow.
- Repeat the request – use the 'broken record' technique to restate the request.
- Be prepared to compromise – you are better off getting partial agreement than rejection.
- Realize the other person has the right to refuse – respect the other person's rights.

Give constructive feedback

Giving constructive feedback to others is an important skill for both our professional and personal lives. Whereas criticism is mostly given without the intention of helping the other person, constructive feedback is aimed at helping them to function better. A model for providing constructive feedback which I have found extremely useful is one that I adapted from the DESC script popularized by Bower and Bower (1976). DESC stands for describe, express, specify, and consequences. This is a technique which professionals find valuable in giving feedback to parents of children with disabilities and also to their colleagues, and which, in addition, parents find extremely useful in handling difficulties with professionals. The four steps involved in using the modified DESC script are described below.

Describe Describe the behaviour of concern in the most specific and objective terms possible. For example, 'When you change teaching programmes without consulting me . . .'.

Express or explain Either express your feelings about this behaviour or explain the difficulties it causes for you, or do both, calmly and positively, without blaming or judging the other person, or 'putting them down'. For example, 'I get very annoyed' (express) 'because parents may become confused and even lose confidence in us' (explain).

Specify Specify the exact change in behaviour required of the other person. For example, '. . . So, in future, will you make sure you consult me before making such changes . . .'.

Consequences The consequences which are likely to result from the other person complying with the request are stated. The benefits for both people are stated first along with any concessions which you are willing to make. For example, 'Then, we will be able to maintain our excellent working relationship and parents will be clear about our teaching programmes'.

If the other person is not willing to comply, then the modified DESC script should be repeated at progressively higher muscle levels, with the highest muscle level including the negative consequences for the person of not complying with the request. For example, 'If you do not consult me as I suggest then I will have to insist on all your teaching plans being formally submitted to me for approval'.

Preparation and delivery Although the modified DESC script is simple enough to be thought up and delivered on the spot it is usually best to write it out beforehand. It is then possible to make sure that the wording is the most appropriate and also to rehearse it with a third person in order to get feedback on it. It can then be decided when, where and how it will be delivered.

Problem-solving

Often teachers find that their opinions differ from those of parents or their colleagues. This can lead to a deterioration in relationships unless these difficulties are resolved. Bolton (1979) has proposed a model for collaboration in solving problems which is useful in this situation. The six steps of the model are described below.

(1) Define problem in terms of needs of each person. This involves the use of active listening in order to clarify the other person's needs and, if possible, to understand the reason for these needs. It also involves stating one's own needs assertively. This is a key element of the model and may take up half of the total time required for the process.
(2) Brainstorming possible solutions. Once both persons' needs are understood brainstorming can be used to seek solutions which meet both sets of needs. First, as many potential solutions as possible should be listed, without attempting to evaluate or clarify any of them. Wild ideas should be included as these often spark off more creative solutions. Then, each other's ideas should be expanded on and clarified.
(3) Select solutions which meet both party's needs. A choice is then made from the list of potential solutions, the one which best meets the needs of both parties. This will probably involve discussing the relative merits of several solutions in meeting each other's needs.

(4)   Plan who will do what, where and by when. It may be useful to make a written note of the decision about what each party will do, where it wi'l be done and when it will be completed.

(5)   Implement the plan. It is clearly important that each party should attempt to follow the agreement closely in implementing the plan.

(6)   Evaluate the process and the solution. An essential part of the problem-solving process is to agree a time when both parties can meet to evaluate how well the solution is meeting each of their needs.

COUNSELLING SKILLS

The counselling model which is proposed for use with parents is based on a general approach to counselling which can be used with children and adults in a wide variety of situations. The model involves a three-stage approach to counselling with stages of listening, understanding, and action planning. It is a problem-solving approach to counselling adapted from previous models by Egan (1982) and Allan and Nairne (1984) and is presented in more detail elsewhere (Hornby, 1994b).

As was suggested earlier in this chapter, *some* parents of children with special needs will be in need of counselling. However, the majority of these parents will not ask for counselling directly, but will typically go to teachers with concerns about their children. If teachers use listening skills in order to help parents explore their concerns then the parents' need for help will emerge. This is when teachers should be able to help parents by providing the counselling that they need. Parents of children with special needs are much more likely to be willing to talk about their concerns with someone who is working directly with their child, such as a therapist or teacher, than with a professional counsellor whom they do not know. What teachers need therefore is a counselling model which is practical, simple to learn and easy to use. A summary of the counselling model proposed is presented in Figure 5.1.

The rationale for using such a model is based on the idea that any problem or concern which parents bring to counselling can be dealt with by taking them through the three stages of the model in order to help them find the solution that best suits their needs. First of all, the teacher uses the skills of the *listening* stage to establish a working relationship with parents, to help them open up and to explore any concerns they have. Then the teacher moves on to the second stage, using the skills of the *understanding* stage in order to help parents get a clearer picture of their concerns, develop new perspectives on

STAGE	LISTENING	UNDERSTANDING	ACTION PLANNING
SKILLS	Attentiveness	Structuring	Brainstorming options
		Summarizing	Evaluating options
	Passive listening	Identifying themes	Action planning skills
		Expressing implications	
	Paraphrasing	Information-giving	Assertion skills
		Suggesting alternative interpretations	
		Suggesting new perspectives	Reviewing skills
	Active listening	Goal-setting	Termination skills

Direction of movement in counselling process

⟶

Figure 5.1 *Counselling model*

their situation, and suggest possible goals for change. Finally, the teacher moves on to the third stage, of *action planning*, in which possible options for solving parents' problems are examined and plans for action are developed. Thus, different skills are needed at each stage of the model: skills for listening in the first stage, skills for understanding in the second stage and skills for action planning in the third stage. These are discussed below.

Skills for listening

The first stage of the model involves the use of the listening skills which were described earlier in this chapter. *Attentiveness* and *passive listening* are used to establish a rapport in order to help parents open up. *Paraphrasing* and *active listening* are used to help parents explore their concerns and ideas.

Skills for understanding

The second stage of the model involves the use of skills designed to increase the parent's understanding of their problem situation. Skills used to help parents get a clearer picture of their concerns include: *structuring*, which involves keeping parents focused on key aspects of their concern; *summarizing*, which involves feeding back to parents an overview of their key thoughts and feelings; *identifying themes*, which involves feeding back to parents any common themes, connections or contradictions running through their account of the problem situation; *expressing implications*, which involves drawing tentative conclusions about the parent's situation and linking this with the possible implications of these conclusions; and *information giving*, which involves teachers sharing with parents, either from their experience of children with special needs or from other knowledge relevant to the parent's situation.

Skills used to help parents develop new perspectives on their situation include: *suggesting alternative interpretations*, which involves suggesting objective explanations for past events to counter the negative interpretations which parents are sometimes held back by; and *suggesting new perspectives*, which involves helping parents to consider more constructive ways of viewing their situation.

Finally, in order to help parents develop possible goals for change, the skill of *goal-setting* is used. This involves helping parents decide on the major aspect of their situation which needs to be focused on and considering potential changes which are desirable and feasible.

Skills for action planning

The third stage of the model involves the use of action planning skills in order to help parents consider possible options for solving their problems, develop plans for action and review the progress of these plans.

The skills used to help parents consider possible options for change are the same ones used in the problem-solving model discussed earlier in this chapter. They include the skills of *brainstorming options* and *evaluating options*.

Once parents have decided on their preferred option, *action planning* skills are used to help them develop concrete plans for implementing this option. In addition, parents may be taught some of the *assertion* skills, discussed earlier in this chapter, in order to help them implement this plan.

Next, *reviewing* skills are used in order to help parents to review the progress of these plans. This involves arranging for further contact in order to evaluate parents' progress with their plans. If there has been insufficient progress then the process can be re-cycled and parents once more taken through the three stages of the model in order to develop a new action plan.

Finally, *termination* skills are used in order to refer parents on for more specialist help, or to bring to a close a successful series of contacts, while communicating to parents that they are welcome to return to discuss other concerns or ideas at any stage in the future.

SUMMARY AND CONCLUSIONS

It has been proposed that teachers need to have good interpersonal communication skills in order to work effectively with parents. Listening, assertion and counselling skills have therefore been elaborated in this chapter. The skills required for effective listening which are discussed include attentiveness, passive listening, paraphrasing and active listening. The assertion skills which are described include techniques for making and refusing requests, giving constructive feedback, handling criticism and problem-solving. The basic counselling skills which are discussed are set within a three-stage problem-solving model of counselling which involves listening, understanding and action planning skills.

Some recent research suggests that teachers are generally more competent at the skills involved in Stages 2 and 3 of this model, which focus on understanding and action planning, than they are at the skills involved in Stage 1, which involves listening (Hornby, 1990; Hornby and Peshawaria, 1991). However, the same research showed that these teachers were able to significantly improve their listening skills and thereby become competent in using the three-stage model with parents in a 30-hour in-service training course. Therefore, it is not unreasonable to expect all teachers of children with special needs to develop competence in these interpersonal skills. Possession of high levels of the skills discussed in this chapter will enable teachers to work effectively with parents using the wide range of communication strategies which are discussed in the following chapter.

6

Communicating with parents

INTRODUCTION

When I got the job of teaching a special class of pupils with moderate learning difficulties in a secondary school in New Zealand I was advised by the previous teacher to visit all of the pupils' parents in their homes as soon as I could. Looking back, this turned out to be probably the best piece of advice I have ever received during my career in education. There were 14 pupils in my class and I made arrangements to visit all their parents at home within the first few weeks of term.

In 13 cases I spent time in my pupils' homes meeting other members of their family and talking with their parents. In one case, my knock on the door was followed by it being opened a couple of inches by what appeared to be my pupil's father. I said who I was and why I had come and the door was firmly closed. In fact, I never had any contact with this boy's parents. I subsequently found out that there were twelve children in the family, one of whom was in jail, that others had been in trouble with the police and that the father could not read or write, factors which may have accounted for his reluctance to let me in.

So although there was one of my pupils' parents whom I never met, these initial home visits laid the foundations for a close working relationship between myself and the other 13 sets of parents. Most of our contacts were by telephone, although we did have annual parents' evenings, which most parents attended and I did make occasional home visits, as is illustrated by the incidents with Grant and Stephen which were mentioned in Chapter 1. Typically, whenever I had a concern about pupils I would telephone their parents in the evening and discuss it with them. Similarly, if they had any concerns they would telephone me at home. In that way any problems which the children presented, either at home or at school, were dealt with by their parents and teacher working together. The pupils soon became aware of this partnership and would often ask 'What were you talking about with my parents last night on the phone?'

I feel certain that the pupils' awareness of the close working relationship I had with their parents helped to avert many potential behaviour problems both at school and at home. This partnership also allowed me to prompt parents to encourage their children to become as independent as possible, as is illustrated by my work with Grant's parents, which is described in Chapter 1.

The experiences I had while working with the parents of my pupils with moderate learning difficulties convinced me of the immense benefits for teachers of establishing effective two-way communication with parents. These experiences initiated my interest in working with parents and in developing strategies for communicating effectively with them. This chapter reviews the wide variety of strategies available to teachers for communicating with parents.

PARENT PREFERENCES

The limited amount of research which has focused on parental preferences has generally found that most parents prefer communication with teachers to be frequent and informal (Turnbull and Turnbull, 1986). Support for this finding was recently obtained from a survey of contact between home and school which was conducted with 72 parents of children attending a special school for children with physical disabilities in the North of England (Young, 1991). This found that 46 per cent of parents had contact with the school at least weekly and 83 per cent had contact at least monthly. With regard to the preferred types of home–school communication, 69 per cent of parents wanted this to be by means of parent–teacher interviews, 67 per cent by telephone calls, 50 per cent by home visits, 47 per cent by home–school diaries and 40 per cent by means of letters. It was reassuring to note that when these parents were asked about the actual forms of contact which they had with staff at the school the percentages for the various types of contact were very similar to those above, except in the area of home visits. Surprisingly, only 15 per cent of parents had received home visits whereas 50 per cent of parents indicated that they would have appreciated them.

Turnbull and Turnbull (1986) reported the results of a survey conducted in the USA with 217 parents of children with a wide range of special needs. This found that 69 per cent of parents wanted to communicate with teachers by means of letters, 51 per cent by parent–teacher interviews, 45 per cent by telephone calls and only 19 per cent by home visits. When another group of parents in the USA were asked to rank 20 different common methods of home–school communication the most popular methods were: directly approaching teachers by telephone or in person; and parent–teacher interviews (Cattermole and Robinson, 1985).

It is clear from the findings of these surveys that there are a few common strategies, but also differences among parents regarding their preferred methods of communicating with teachers. Therefore, it is important for schools to be able to offer parents a range of communication options. However, teachers must also consider their own needs and those of their families in deciding the types of strategies they are prepared to use. As I mentioned earlier, when I taught the special class I was happy to communicate with parents mostly through telephone calls and home visits, nearly all of which occurred in the evening. At that time I had no children of my own. Now that I have children I would probably need to place some limits on these strategies and make more use of other forms of communication.

There are five main methods for developing and maintaining two-way communication between parents and teachers: informal contacts; parent–teacher meetings; home visits; telephone contacts; and various forms of written communication. These are now discussed in turn, starting with informal contacts.

INFORMAL CONTACTS

Informal contacts are a useful way of 'breaking the ice' in most forms of human relationships and this is also the case in relationships with parents. Such contacts provide a means whereby parents and teachers can meet each other as people with a mutual interest in building relationships on behalf of children, thereby helping to break down the barriers that often exist between school and home (Swap, 1993). Informal contacts are particularly important for parents of children newly enrolled at the school or when there has not been a high level of parent involvement at the school in the past. In the latter situation, teachers understandably become despondent when the attendance at more formal events, such as parents' evenings, is so poor. When this is the case it is often best to organize informal events in order to increase the numbers of parents having contact with the school and thereby establish the context necessary for the development of other forms of contact.

The organization of informal contacts is illustrated by the following descriptions of four different types of activities: school productions; open days; gala days; and outings into the local community.

School productions

The type of informal occasion guaranteed to achieve the maximum attendance of parents is one in which they see their children perform in some way or other. In special schools it is possible to organize activities so that all pupils are involved in such events as nativity plays and thereby ensure almost 100 per cent attendance of parents. In mainstream schools this is much more difficult and other strategies are needed.

Open days

Another way to encourage a large proportion of parents to come into the school is to have an 'open day' or 'open evening' when parents can come along to see classes in progress and/or displays of their children's work.

Outings

Class or year-group or even school outings to places such as local parks at weekends or holiday times can attract large numbers of parents and other family members.

Gala days

Events whose main aim is raising funds for the school, by having stalls which sell home-made food and activities such as coconut shies, also provide opportunities for teachers, parents and pupils to meet informally.

Ensuring success of informal events

Swap (1993) provides a list of suggestions for making informal occasions successful. These are outlined below.

Personal invitations In addition to the event being advertised in the school newsletter, parents should receive individually addressed invitations, possibly produced and delivered by their children. Invitations should give at least two weeks' notice of the event, preferably a month, so that parents can make the necessary arrangements. Then, two or three days before the event, reminder notes should be sent home with the children.

Facilitating attendance The two major difficulties which parents experience in arranging to attend school events are with transportation and child care. Providing assistance in each of these areas will improve attendance rates. For example, organizing car pools or minibuses to pick up parents will enable some parents to come who otherwise would not have been able to. Also, organizing child care facilities or making the event suitable for the whole family to attend is likely to increase attendance substantially. Finally, it is worth bearing in mind that events planned for evenings and weekends are more likely to get fathers involved.

Welcoming atmosphere The first step taken in any form of parental involvement should be to make parents feel welcome. For events held at the school it is important to make the school entrance and foyer as welcoming and comfortable as possible. Ideally, when parents first arrive they should be greeted and shown around by pupils or other parents. If this is not possible then directions to where the event is to be held should be clearly signposted.

Optimizing opportunities for informal communication Careful planning is required to ensure that informal events do provide opportunities for parents and teachers to mix and talk with each other. Seating arrangements and planned activities should be organized to facilitate mixing rather than allowing people to sit with others they already know.

Providing food and drink One of the best ways of promoting informal conversation is through arranging for food and drink at an event. There is something about eating and drinking with other people which helps to cement relationships and build rapport. Pot-luck meals when everyone brings a plate of home-cooked food are particularly good for this.

Evaluating activities Inviting parents to formally and informally evaluate activities ensures that their feedback can be used to improve subsequent events.

HOME VISITS

As noted earlier in this chapter, many parents appreciate it when their children's teachers are prepared to come and visit them on their own territory. Such home visits can be pivotal in establishing close working relationships with parents. They enable teachers to see for themselves the circumstances in which the family are living. They also enable teachers to meet other members of the family such as siblings and fathers whom they may not otherwise meet. Knowledge of these factors can help teachers understand how their pupils may be affected by the home situation.

Home visits also enable teachers to find out how their pupils spend their time at home, whether they have any hobbies, how much television they watch and what time they usually go to bed. It is also possible to find out how pupils behave at home and how their parents handle them. Finally, home visits provide an opportunity for teachers to answer parents' questions and deal with any concerns they may have.

Because making home visits had paid such dividends for me as a special class teacher I expected that most teachers of children with special needs who were in special schools or units in mainstream schools would make visits to their pupils' homes. I was therefore surprised to learn, from a survey of special education teachers conducted in Auckland a few years ago, that this was not the case. This New Zealand survey revealed that less than 10 per cent of parents of children in special classes in mainstream schools had received home visits from their children's teachers. Further evidence for the low level of home visiting carried out by teachers of children with special needs was provided by the results of the recent survey of parents whose children attended a special school in the North of England. As reported above, Young (1991) found that only 15 per cent of these parents had received home visits.

The reasons for the low priority given to home visiting by teachers of children with special needs are hard to assess. It is possible that teachers are generally not aware of how much many parents appreciate receiving home visits from their children's teachers. Also, teachers may not realize the benefits which can accrue for them and their pupils from making such home visits. There are also difficulties for teachers with families themselves in making home visits, since in most cases this would need to be done in the evening because they are teaching all day. In recognition of this problem and the value to children of improving relationships between school and home, some LEAs have set up Home–School Liaison schemes. The scheme in Humberside involves selected primary schools having a teacher half of whose time is used to release class teachers during the school day so that they can make home visits to the parents of children whose progress or behaviour is causing a concern.

In contrast, many secondary schools still actively discourage classroom teachers from having contacts with parents other than on 'parents' evenings'. But this is certainly not true of them all. For example, one secondary school in a socially deprived area of Hull is well known for ensuring that visits are made to the homes of all their new intake of pupils before they begin each year. The visits are made by the teachers and senior teachers who will be involved with the new intake of pupils and are considered to have significantly reduced the level of behavioural problems at the school.

Guidelines for home visits

In order to optimize the effectiveness of home visits certain guidelines should be followed (Seligman, 1979). These are outlined below.

Arranging visits Home visits should always be prearranged since some parents might be embarrassed about the lack of tidiness and cleanliness of their house if teachers just arrived unannounced. It is usually best for teachers to write letters to parents saying that they wish to make home visits to the parents of all their pupils and will be phoning in the next few days to make arrangements with those parents who would like this.

Dress Since in their own homes parents will be dressed casually, it is best if teachers dress less formally than they do at school so that parents will feel more at ease. Some parents may find it more difficult to open up with a teacher dressed in a suit and tie when they are wearing their fluffy carpet slippers!

Time It is clearly best to arrange to visit at a time of day when all the family members will be present and when parents will have a chance to talk. For most families, the middle of the evening, when families have finished their evening meal, is the best time. It is important to be punctual and to allow sufficient time for the visit. It is also important not to stay too long as parents will need time to get the children ready for bed and possibly do other chores ready for the morning. It is usually best to allow visits to last for from one to two hours but to set a limit half an hour before your actual deadline to cope with the phenomenon that parents will mention their greatest concern just as you are leaving!

Courtesy It is important to respect the hospitality associated with the cultural group from which the family comes. With most English families this will simply mean accepting the offer of a cup of tea or coffee but for West Indian families it will probably mean accepting something to eat as well. When I was teaching in New Zealand and made a home visit to a Samoan family I found that they had prepared a full meal of Samoan food all served on banana leaves for my arrival. Fortunately, I had been forewarned that it is not possible to discuss important matters in a Samoan household until you have eaten with the family.

Listening Throughout the visit teachers need to be aware of using the listening skills discussed in Chapter 5 in order to help parents express their priorities and concerns about their children with special needs.

Questions Teachers will want to ask parents for information about their children, such as about any medical problems or about their behaviour at home. It is also important to give parents time to ask questions of the teacher.

Distractions Teachers should anticipate that there are likely to be distractions during the visit and be determined not to become irritated by them.

TELEPHONE CONTACTS

Nowadays the vast majority of parents have a telephone but when there is a child with special needs in the family it is even more important to be on the phone. This is partly because there is more often a need for urgent medical assistance to be summoned and partly because such families tend to be more restricted in their ability to leave the home. So most parents of children with special needs are quite comfortable about communicating by telephone. Also, as noted earlier in this chapter, many parents prefer to communicate with teachers by means of the telephone.

Parents phoning teachers

Many parents appreciate the opportunity of being able to phone teachers directly either at school or at home. However, there are difficulties associated with both of these options. The main problem with parents phoning teachers at school is that teachers should only have to leave their class to answer the telephone in absolute emergencies. So it is usually best to get the school secretary to take messages and tell parents that the teacher will phone back as soon as possible.

Some teachers may not be prepared to allow parents to phone them at home. This is perfectly understandable since they may feel the need to have some time to themselves, or with their own families, which work pressures do not impinge on. Other teachers may want to encourage parents to phone them at home in preference to being phoned at school. An alternative solution is to set a specified time of day or evening during the week when parents know the teacher will be at home and available to answer the phone.

Teachers phoning parents

As mentioned at the start of this chapter, the communication channel which I used most frequently when teaching the special class was to telephone parents at home in the evening. With hindsight I would probably use this option less and employ a wider range of the strategies described here, in order to cater for different preferences among parents and to use my leisure time more efficiently. However, phoning parents at home paid such high dividends in maintaining productive relationships with parents that I would always want to include it in my range of strategies for communicating with parents. Alternatively, teachers may like to check whether some parents are at home during the day and others are happy to be phoned at work, in which case at least some of the calls could be made from school during the day.

Whenever telephone calls are made to parents there are certain guidelines which it is wise to follow. The following guidelines were generated from reflecting on some of my successes and errors in phoning parents and from adapting the suggestions made by Turnbull and Turnbull (1986).

(1) Identify yourself as their child's teacher when parents first answer.

(2) Ask if it is a convenient time to talk or whether it would be better if you called back later.

(3) Make a point of finding out the best time to call parents. Usually later in the evening, when children are in bed, is the most suitable time.

(4) Use a written list of things you want to ask or tell parents which you have prepared beforehand.

(5) Be concise and to the point. If an issue needs lengthy discussion it is better to do it face to face rather than on the phone.

(6) Listen carefully to what the parent has to say, using the listening skills discussed in Chapter 5.

(7) Give the parent time to ask you questions and to think about the things you have said.

(8) If you don't have the information that parents want, suggest you will find out and get back to them as soon as possible.

(9)   Avoid relaying sensitive information by telephone. This is better done face to face so that parents' reactions can be gauged.
(10) Always finish by thanking parents for their time and remind them that they can contact you any time they have a concern.

Other uses of the telephone

Two other uses of the telephone in working with parents are reported by Turnbull and Turnbull (1986). First, the telephone tree can be used as an efficient way to get information to parents. Once the list (or tree) of parents' names and phone numbers is circulated to all parents the teacher simply has to ring the first name on the list and parents then ring each other in turn to pass on the information. Variations on this system include the teacher phoning two parents who in turn phone another two parents. This continues until all parents have been contacted. An additional benefit of the telephone tree is that parents are encouraged to interact with one another which may lead to supportive friendships being formed.

Second, an answerphone can be used to play recorded daily messages for parents who ring the school phone number in the evening or at the weekend. For example, messages can be recorded to tell parents about the activities the class have been involved in during the day, about the homework that has been set or to remind them about equipment needed for the following day. Turnbull and Turnbull report a study which found that children performed better on homework tasks using the system of recorded daily messages rather than the traditional homework diaries.

WRITTEN COMMUNICATION

As mentioned at the beginning of this chapter, many parents prefer to communicate with teachers by means of letters. Other parents find that home–school diaries are the best means of keeping them in contact with the school. In addition, newsletters and handbooks written especially for parents of children with special needs can keep parents in touch with what is happening at school. It is therefore clear that the written word provides an important means of communication between teachers and parents.

However, there are two major difficulties with this form of communication. First, if some of the pupils' parents do not have English as their first language then ideally every written communication to parents needs to be translated into their own languages. Second, it is important to remember that some parents have reading difficulties themselves. Therefore, written materials cannot be relied upon to communicate effectively with all parents. This also suggests that all written materials should use language which is simple and able to be understood by the majority of parents.

Handbooks

Most schools have prospectuses or brochures whose purpose is to inform new or prospective parents about the school's aims and organization. These tend to be general documents which focus on promoting positive features of the school and informing parents about the major school rules for pupils and policies for teaching (Bastiani, 1989). It has been suggested by Kroth (1985) that parents of children with special needs appreciate having a handbook written especially for them. The handbook should inform parents about their rights and responsibilities regarding their children along with all the information they need in order to help them to be happy and successful at the school. For parents of children with special needs in ordinary schools a handbook prepared for all parents who have children at the school may be able to meet their needs if it addresses the following aspects of school life.

Personnel School staff, especially heads of year and the school's co-ordinator for special educational needs, should be listed along with their contact phone numbers, as well as those of outside specialists such as educational psychologists and services for children with sensory losses.

Policies The school's policy for parental involvement and for meeting special needs should be clearly spelled out. These should include an explanation for parents of whom to contact if they have a concern and of the best methods for making this contact.

School-wide procedures School rules regarding dress and discipline should be briefly outlined and the specific procedures for rewarding effort and progress and for dealing with misbehaviour should be explained.

Classroom procedures An indication of the materials and equipment pupils will need for various subjects should be included.

Transport The arrangements for transporting pupils to and from school should be detailed.

Reports home A description of the type and frequency of the progress reports parents will receive should be included.

Other information Any other information which would be helpful to parents should be included, such as details of Adult Education classes relevant to parenting which are based at the school.

Newsletters

Newsletters regularly sent out to parents, typically once a term, are a very good way of communicating with the majority of parents. Newsletters can be general ones which are addressed to all parents of children at the school, or more specific ones addressed to parents of children in a particular year, or just to the parents of children with special needs. Newsletters can include a variety of content such as notices for forthcoming events, updates of ongoing school projects and invitations for parents to help at the school.

Letters and notes

Letters are a time-consuming means for communicating with parents. Therefore, it is generally better to use the other forms of communication described above for most purposes and only use letters for situations which require a more formal approach. For example, most schools will, as a last resort, use letters to express concern about a child's behaviour and invite parents to come to school to discuss the problem. However, this use of letters to deal with discipline problems should be balanced by a system of positive letters sent to parents to acknowledge a child's outstanding effort or progress.

In contrast to formal letters teachers often find it useful to send brief handwritten notes home to parents via children's school bags. This can be a quick and effective way of getting a message to parents with whom teachers already have a good relationship, but it does have its drawbacks. Notes can sometimes become lost on the way home or can be overlooked when parents are emptying the school bag. Also, there is no record kept of what has been written.

Home–school diary

Many parents prefer to use a book for written communication between themselves and teachers. It is more difficult for a book to be overlooked or lost, it provides a record of messages sent home and it allows parents to write a message back to the teacher if they so wish. However, some parents are reluctant to write notes back to the teacher because they do not want to expose their weaknesses in spelling or grammar. Others may think that they have little of value to write back to the teacher about. So teachers should accept that although they encourage all parents to reply to their comments in home–school diaries, parents will vary in their use of this opportunity. Simply because parents do not write in the diary does not mean that they don't value it; the vast majority of them do.

In special schools and units for children with special needs home–school diaries are typically sent home daily with each child. But this is not always the case and in some schools they are sent home at the end of the week, while in others they are only used for selected pupils. Therefore, there is no reason why home–school diaries should not be used for children with special needs who have been integrated into mainstream classes, even if the child is the only one with such a book.

The home–school diary can be used to exchange information with parents on a wide variety of subjects. For example, it can be used to let parents know about children's accomplishments at school, or a note can be made of the topics discussed and activities carried out by children at school so that this can be discussed by parents at home. Alternatively, what children have done at home during the evening or the weekend or the holidays can be noted by parents so that the teacher can follow up these topics at school. Similarly, parents can inform teachers about any circumstances at home which may have upset their child, while teachers can let parents know about any misbehaviour which has occurred at school. However, it is best not to communicate essentially sensitive or negative information by means of the diary. This is better done face to face, as mentioned earlier.

Turnbull and Turnbull (1986) suggest that parents should be involved in deciding what information is included in the diary as well as how often it will be sent home and whether parents want to write in it. In my experience, when parents do decide to write in the diary this method of communication generally works very well and makes a significant contribution to strengthening relationships between the parents and teachers concerned.

A variation on the home–school book, recently suggested by Sicley (1993), is the weekly folder. This is simply a manilla folder in which a sheet of paper with a line down the middle is stapled. At the end of the week the teacher writes a brief message for parents on the left-hand side of the sheet and encloses in the folder notices, newsletters, details of homework or samples of the pupils' work for their parents to see. When the folder is taken home parents then have the opportunity to write a comment on the sheet next to the teacher's message. When the sheets get filled up new ones are stapled on top of the old ones so that a record of the messages can be kept. In this way, the weekly folder provides a quick and efficient method for maintaining contact with parents and keeping them in touch with what their children are doing at school.

Progress reports

Reports on children's progress are the most longstanding and widely used form of written communication to parents. However, such reports have been undergoing some changes in recent years. A type of report which has become very popular with schools is the Record of Achievement (ROA). Although each school develops its own format, ROAs have several common components. First, they list the major achievements made by the pupil in each subject area. Second, pupils comment on these achievements and on their satisfaction with their progress in each subject and on any specific weaknesses they have. Third, pupils state their immediate goals in each subject. Fourth, teachers comment on pupils' achievements and on their immediate goals. Finally, ROAs are then sent out to parents. This is done once a year in most schools but twice or three times a year in some.

However, many parents have been frustrated by the tremendous amount of detail in ROAs and the absence of information which would enable them to compare their children's progress with that of other children of their age. It is perhaps because of parents' dissatisfaction with some aspects of ROAs that statutory guidance on progress reports has recently been published (DFE, 1993). This guidance requires schools to:

- report to parents on their children's progress at least annually
- report on progress in all subjects and activities at school
- report on overall progress and on attendance
- report how the results of assessments on National Curriculum subjects compare with the results of other children of the same age in the school.

PARENT–TEACHER MEETINGS

The form of contact with parents with which all teachers are familiar is that of parents' evenings or parent–teacher interviews. These meetings are a well-established method of involving parents and not without reason, as research has shown that they have an impact on both parent–teacher relationships and pupil progress (Turnbull and Turnbull, 1986). It has been found that children whose parents attend such meetings have higher attendance rates, fewer behaviour problems and improved academic achievement. Of course experienced teachers would immediately suggest that this is because the parents of 'good kids' usually attend parents' evenings whereas parents of pupils with behavioural or learning difficulties tend not to turn up. However, as noted in Chapter 2, it must not be assumed that parents who do not turn up to parents' evenings are not interested in their children's education. There is a variety of reasons why some parents do not attend such meetings, including transport and babysitting problems, as well as parents' negative feelings about their own schooldays. Perhaps if these problems could be overcome then these parents would come to parents' evenings and this would lead to better parent–teacher relationships and thereby an improvement in their children's behaviour and progress at school. I believe that it would, but it is usually easier to use other strategies to communicate with these parents rather than overcome the problems. By using either home visits, telephone contacts or written communication good parent–teacher relationships can be established which should lead to improvements in children's behaviour and academic progress.

However, it is typically only a minority of parents who don't come to parents' evenings. Regular parent–teacher meetings are desired by the majority of parents as was noted earlier. The fact that nearly all schools hold such meetings suggests that teachers also find that they are a useful way of communicating between home and school. Bastiani (1989) has suggested that teachers and parents have different goals for such meetings.

Teachers' goals include:

- informing parents of their children's progress
- establishing good relationships with parents
- telling parents about the difficulties their children have at school
- checking with parents how their children are coping with school
- learning more about children, from parents' perspectives
- finding out parents' opinions about the school programme
- identifying ways in which parents can help their children at home
- identifying potential conflicts between parents and teachers
- jointly making decisions about children's education.

Parents' goals include:

- meeting all the people who teach their children
- finding out about their children's progress
- finding out about any difficulties they are having
- passing on important information about their children

- questioning teachers about any concerns they have
- finding out ways of helping their children at home
- comparing their child's progress with that of others in the class
- discussing any difficulties which they are experiencing at home
- learning more about the school and the methods of teaching used.

Swap (1993) has suggested that an important hidden agenda which parents have at such meetings is to check whether the teacher really knows and understands their child.

Whatever goals teachers and parents have for these meetings it is important to both participants that they are organized to ensure effective communication. Several authors have provided suggestions for optimizing the effectiveness of parent–teacher meetings (Kroth, 1985; Simpson, 1990; Swap, 1993; Turnbull and Turnbull, 1986). It is from these that the following guidelines are drawn. The guidelines are divided into three sections focusing on tasks for before and after meetings as well as those for actually conducting the meetings.

Organizing parent–teacher meetings

On parents' evenings, because of the typically large number of parents each teacher has to meet, there is considerable time pressure on parent–teacher interviews. It is therefore important to do as much as possible beforehand to ensure that time in the meeting is used as effectively as possible. The following guidelines are suggested with this aim in mind. They will also apply to additional individual parent–teacher interviews which are set up at the request of either parents or teachers.

Making initial contacts It is of course preferable if the teacher's first contact with parents is not in a formal parent–teacher interview. It is far better if the initial contact is made by means of a home visit or one of the informal forms of contact discussed earlier. However, this is not always possible, so for many parents this formal situation will be their first contact with their child's teacher.

Notifying parents Notifying parents about parent–teacher meetings is usually best done by letters of invitation sent home at least two weeks in advance, if possible followed up by less formal reminders two or three days beforehand. Reminders can be a brief note in a child's school bag or a short telephone call. Invitations need to specify the place, time and length of time allotted for the meeting.

The purpose of the meeting should be made quite clear and in a non-threatening way so that parents do not worry unnecessarily.

Helping parents prepare Along with the invitation parents can be sent some guidelines to help them prepare for the meeting. Kroth (1985) suggests that most parents appreciate this because it conveys a message that parental input is welcome at the meeting. Guidelines for parents could include:

- making a list of questions to ask or concerns to raise e.g. about the child's progress in various subjects, behaviour in class and in the playground, relationships with teachers and other children
- being prepared to ask for clarification of any unfamiliar terminology which the teacher uses
- being prepared to comment on children's activities at home e.g. hobbies, interests and amount of TV watched
- being prepared to comment on the way children are disciplined at home and what limits are set e.g. regarding TV viewing, homework completion and bedtime
- being prepared to comment on factors which may affect children's learning e.g. child's health, health of other family members, any other relevant family circumstances
- talking to children to check whether they have any concerns about school or questions they would like the teacher to be asked.

Preparing room Since physical environment has an impact on the quality of communication in meetings it is important to book the most suitable venue available. Typically the teacher's classroom will be used and this need not be inappropriate as long as certain basic steps are taken. For example, the most comfortable chairs available should be found and arranged so that there are no physical barriers, such as desks, between parents and the teacher. Also, distractions should be avoided and privacy maintained by keeping the classroom door closed and having a 'Do Not Disturb' sign on the outside of it.

Reviewing children's work Before the meeting it is useful to review children's records, assessment data and work done at school. Typical examples of children's work can be selected in order to show parents at the meeting.

Involving other staff Where relevant it is also important to talk with other members of staff who work with the children in order to obtain more information and get their views on the children's progress.

Involving children Where appropriate, children can be involved in the meeting along with their parents. If this is not considered appropriate then the child should be told about the purpose of the meeting and given the opportunity to have input into the agenda.

Preparing agenda A list of issues needing to be raised with parents should be made and these should be ranked in order of priority so that key concerns can be dealt with first. It may not be possible to cover all of the issues since parents are likely to want time to discuss items of concern to them.

Conducting parent–teacher meetings

Although the focus of meetings is necessarily on the issues to be discussed it must not be forgotten that establishing effective working relationships with parents is more important in the long term. So the manner in which meetings are conducted is of vital importance. It has been suggested that, in the past, parent–teacher meetings have been characterized by a one-way flow of information, from teacher to parent (Simpson, 1990). However, as noted earlier, relationships between parents and teachers can only be successful if there is a two-way communication process which involves sharing information, concerns and ideas (Chinn *et al.*, 1978). Therefore, in order to conduct effective meetings with parents, teachers need to use many of the interpersonal skills which were discussed in Chapter 5, plus those which are referred to below.

Rapport building When parents first arrive time should be spent welcoming them and making them feel at ease. They should be thanked for coming and encouraged to ask questions or comment at any time during the meeting.

Structuring It is always wise to remind parents of the time limits set for the meeting since there is good evidence that setting time limits helps to reduce irrelevant discussions (Simpson, 1990). Then the purpose of the meeting can be stated and the agenda items proposed by the teacher can be listed. Parents should be asked if there are other issues or concerns they would like to discuss at the meeting. Parents' items can then be added to the agenda which should be dealt with in agreed priority order.

Note-taking It is easier to build rapport in a meeting if notes are not taken during it. However, teachers often find it useful to note important details and list things they need to do after the meeting.

Parents may also want to make notes. So the issue of note-taking should be discussed at the beginning of the meeting. If teachers explain the reasons for wanting to take notes, are sensitive about what they write down and allow parents to see what they have written, then this should not interfere with the communication process.

Providing information It is usually best to start on a positive note by stating the areas in which the child is doing well. Concerns the teacher has about difficulties the child is experiencing or creating should be stated clearly and specifically but with sensitivity. Parents want teachers to be honest with them but not brutal. If part of the difficulty which teachers need to convey involves providing some negative feedback to parents, for example, if pupils are consistently not doing their homework and parents do not appear to be monitoring this, then the modified DESC script (see Chapter 5) can be used.

Obtaining information In order to get parents to open up and share concerns and ideas teachers need to use the skills of attentiveness, asking open questions, paraphrasing and active listening which were discussed in Chapter 5.

Problem-solving Where specific problems emerge with no obvious solutions or where teachers and parents disagree then the problem-solving procedure, which was discussed in Chapter 5, should be used.

Termination At the end of the meeting teachers should summarize the main points which have emerged and review the action which both parents and teachers have agreed to take. If more time is needed then further meetings should be arranged. Finally, parents should be thanked for their participation and reminded that they can contact the teacher any time they require information or have a concern about their child.

Reviewing parent–teacher meetings

Following the meeting teachers have several tasks to complete in order to make best use of its outcome.

Making a record A brief report should be written to summarize the main issues which were discussed and the decisions which emerged from the meeting. It should record the individuals responsible for carrying out each recommendation which was agreed upon.

Discuss with children A brief review of the items discussed at the meeting should be conducted with the children involved and the impact of any recommendations on them explained. Children should then be given the opportunity to ask questions about the meeting.

Liaise with colleagues Other members of staff should be informed about the outcome of the meeting and any recommendations relevant to their work with the child discussed with them.

Plan for follow-up Teachers need to plan for the implementation of the recommendations agreed at the meeting and for any follow-up meetings which were scheduled.

Evaluate The best way for teachers to get feedback from parents on the effectiveness of the meetings from their perspective is to ask parents to complete a brief questionnaire. Several writers have provided sample questionnaires (see Kroth, 1985; Simpson, 1990; Turnbull and Turnbull, 1986) on which parents are asked to rate aspects of the parent–teacher meeting such as: the suitability of the room used; the adequacy of the time available; the appropriateness of the agenda; the adequacy of information obtained; the quality of the teacher's listening skills; the helpfulness of recommendations.

SUMMARY AND CONCLUSIONS

A range of possible strategies for communicating with parents have been discussed in this chapter. Informal contacts such as open days, school productions and outings were suggested as ways of 'breaking the ice'. The importance of home visits in building relationships with parents was stressed and guidelines for making them were provided. Guidelines were also provided for the use of telephone contacts with parents. Several forms of written communication were considered including handbooks, newsletters, progress reports and home–school diaries. Finally, the organization, conduct and review of parent–teacher meetings was discussed at length. In conclusion, it can be seen that a wide variety of strategies is available to teachers for communicating with parents. The actual methods used will depend on teacher and parent preferences but in general it is considered that making a range of strategies available to parents will result in effective communication with the maximum number of parents.

Parental involvement in their children's education

INTRODUCTION

I first became convinced of the benefits of parents' involvement in their children's education when, as a trainee educational psychologist, a 12-year-old girl who was on the point of being excluded from school was referred to me. Carol was disruptive in class, argued openly with teachers and used foul language as well as frequently having disputes with other pupils in class and in the playground. The most obvious intervention was a behaviour modification programme, designed in collaboration with her teachers, which would be instituted throughout the school day. However, the school were not willing to consider rewards or incentives for Carol over and above those available to other pupils.

A solution to this problem was found by using what have come to be known as 'Home–School Behaviour Programmes' or 'Home–School Notes' (Atkeson and Forehand, 1979; Kelley, 1990). In this intervention Carol's teachers simply recorded the appropriateness of her behaviour on a report form which she took home at the end of the week. Carol's parents were to provide certain incentives, which had been agreed with Carol, depending on the details of the teachers' report on her behaviour over the week. The incentives included staying up half an hour later at night, visiting her grandmother and going swimming.

From the day this programme started Carol's behaviour improved dramatically and she presented no further problems of any significance for the remainder of the school year. The key to this positive outcome was involving Carol's parents in a positive way. In the past, contacts between home and school had consisted mainly of teachers informing the parents about her misdemeanours. Once the programme started teachers were reporting mostly appropriate behaviour so Carol's parents were put in the position of rewarding her for good behaviour. Hence, this form of parental involvement consisted mainly of a structure which enabled Carol's parents to provide support to her teachers in ensuring that she behaved appropriately at school. Although finishing the academic tasks she had been set was one of the criteria listed on Carol's incentive programme, the major focus of her parents' involvement was on her behaviour.

I became convinced of the importance of parental involvement in other aspects of their children's education by the work done by Ted Glynn, who was one of my tutors on a training course in educational psychology, at Auckland University in New Zealand. In the late 1970s and early 1980s Glynn and his colleagues conducted research projects in which parents were trained to help their children with reading at home (Glynn, 1985).

The project which impressed me the most was one which involved five children, and their mothers, who had recently arrived from Cambodia (Glynn and Glynn, 1986). None of the mothers could either read or speak more than a few words of English before the study. They were taught how to use a shared reading procedure (described later in this chapter) in order to help their children to learn to read. The mothers engaged in shared reading sessions with their children every night after school. This was in addition to the school reading programme which the children were following and to small group tuition from the English as a Second Language teacher.

The results of the study showed that, over a period of 24 weeks, the children made gains of from one to two years in their reading attainment. From the research design used it was possible to see that the most dramatic gains in reading ability were made when the shared reading was begun. This result was even more startling because the parents involved were themselves learning to read English along with their children. The findings of this study appear to provide very strong support for the effectiveness of parental involvement in their children's education because if parents who can hardly speak English can facilitate their children's progress through working with them at home, then the potential benefits for all parents to help in this way are clearly substantial.

This chapter will first briefly discuss the effectiveness of parental involvement and then review various approaches to involving parents in the education of their children. The approaches will be considered in approximate chronological order of their development. The first types of parental involvement grew out of the early intervention schemes of the 1960s and 1970s. At about the same time the training of parents in techniques to modify their children's behaviour began to be developed. The 1980s saw the rapid development of schemes designed to involve parents in helping their children to read. These were followed by schemes which focused on other curriculum areas such as mathematics and spelling.

Finally, in the last decade, there has been an increasing impetus to improve the involvement of parents in the assessment of their children and in reviews of their progress.

EFFECTIVENESS OF PARENTAL INVOLVEMENT

Reviews of the literature consistently provide support for the effectiveness of parental involvement in facilitating children's development. Swap (1993) reports that gains are made when parents are involved as supporters of their children's learning or are simply kept informed about their progress at school. However, she states that the greatest gains are made when parents act as tutors with their children. She gives examples of successful projects at preschool, primary and secondary levels for which parental involvement was a major component.

At the pre-school level Swap cites the Perry Preschool Project (Berrueta-Clement *et al.*, 1984) which included one and a half hour weekly home visits for all children in the project and their mothers. Children who participated in the programme had significantly higher IQs than control group children throughout their first two years at school. Although IQ differences disappeared after this a follow-up study revealed that the programme produced important long-term benefits. These included increased academic achievement, decreased need for special education placement, less unemployment and fewer contacts with the criminal justice system. It has been suggested that involving the parents was the key to maintaining the benefits of the programme.

At the primary school level Swap cites a study (Tizard *et al.*, 1982) which compared the effects of parental involvement in their children's reading with the provision of additional specialist tutorial assistance with reading at school. The results showed that primary school children who read aloud to their parents two to four times a week from books sent home from school made significantly greater gains in reading achievement than children receiving additional assistance at school.

Studies of parental involvement at the secondary school level are much less numerous than those of primary or pre-school programmes. Swap cites a study of parent involvement in mathematics in which she was one of the researchers (Moses *et al.*, 1989). The Algebra Project relied heavily on parent involvement in order to improve the achievement of secondary school pupils in mathematics. Parents were involved in the project in several ways: as project leader; through informational meetings; through participation in workshops; and by acting as voluntary classroom helpers. The project produced a substantial improvement in mathematics performance for the students involved compared with the achievement of previous years' students. This result was attributed mainly to the high level of parental involvement in the project.

EARLY INTERVENTION PROJECTS

Early intervention for disadvantaged pre-school children in the USA began in the 1960s under the Headstart project, which was a key element in President Kennedy's 'war on poverty'. A variety of schemes were established in different parts of the country, each with its own approach. The majority of these programmes were centre-based, with parents typically bringing along their children for a few half-day sessions per week. Programmes varied in the extent to which they involved parents, with some having only minimal involvement.

Initial evaluations of the effectiveness of the schemes suggested that large gains in IQ could be achieved. However, follow-up studies found that the IQ gains had generally disappeared after two years of primary schooling so the focus was placed on maintenance of the early gains. Bronfenbrenner's (1976) analysis of the research evidence suggested that the programmes which had higher levels of parent involvement were the ones which produced higher levels of immediate gains and that these gains were more likely to be maintained as children progressed through primary school. Teacher–parent contacts in general and home visits in particular seemed to be associated with more effective programmes. This finding led to increased attention being paid to early intervention projects which were home-based such as the Portage project which is discussed later in this section.

Follow-up studies have showed that early intervention programmes have important long-term effects, as noted above (Berrueta-Clement *et al.*, 1984). It has been estimated that seven dollars are saved for every dollar spent on early intervention because of savings on such things as remedial teaching, special education placements, unemployment benefits, and costs to the criminal justice system. This powerful argument in favour of early intervention and parent involvement has recently been used to support the idea of expanding nursery provision in the UK so that it is available to all pre-school children.

Project High/Scope

One of the programmes which has recently been gaining popularity in the UK is Project High/Scope. This programme evolved from the

Perry Preschool Project (Berrueta-Clement *et al.*, 1984) which was referred to above. The philosophy of High/Scope is based on the work of Piaget and Dewey, so the importance of active learning and children using their initiative are emphasized. The programme has mainly been used with children aged 3 to 5 years and typically involves daily three-hour sessions based at a pre-school centre coupled with weekly home visits. High/Scope has several components which are considered to be essential to its success: child-initiated learning; a structured environment; a daily routine; key experiences; and a high level of parental involvement.

Child-initiated learning occurs because High/Scope teachers provide opportunities for children to learn actively and construct their own knowledge. Children are given control over the learning situation and acquire knowledge through actively experiencing the world around them by choosing, exploring, manipulating and experimenting with the materials provided. The environment is structured so that children have a choice between developmentally appropriate activities which will provide certain key experiences designed to facilitate the development of logical thinking and promote cognitive, social, physical, and emotional development.

A distinctive feature of the programme is the establishment of a daily routine which includes the use of a plan–do–review sequence. At the start of each session children are asked to choose the activities they want to engage in and plan how they will spend their time. In the do phase teachers support, enquire about and extend children's play. At the end of the session children are asked to review their day's play either symbolically or verbally in order to link the planning and doing phases.

The role of parents is regarded as being crucial to the effectiveness of the programme. Therefore, parental participation is encouraged in all aspects of High/Scope. In particular, teachers make weekly home visits of about 90 minutes during which the child's progress is discussed and parents are invited to observe and participate in various activities with their children. Parents are encouraged to see themselves as experts on their children and as partners with teachers in the programme.

Portage project

During the late 1960s, early intervention programmes began to be established for children with delayed development. The best known of these is the Portage project which was established in Portage, Wisconsin in 1969 (Shearer and Shearer, 1972). The Portage programme is designed to help parents, and possibly other members of their extended family, to teach their children at home.

A major aim of the programme is to develop parents' skills so that they can work with their children within the home. The programme has five components: a check-list of developmental skills; teaching cards; activity charts; a book of readings; and home visits from a Portage worker.

The Portage check-list consists of 580 items divided into six colour-coded areas of development: cognitive skills; language skills; social skills; fine and gross motor skills; activities of daily living; plus a section on infant stimulation. In each area the items are ordered in approximate developmental sequence for children from birth to six years. The check-list is initially used by the Portage worker to assess the child in each of the six areas of development. Through a combination of discussion with the parents and observation of the child the items on the check-list which the child has already accomplished are ticked off. The check-list items just beyond those ticked then provide ideas for aspects of the child's development which should be taught next.

The teaching cards each have a check-list item written as a behavioural objective along with suggestions of how to teach this skill. The cards are sequenced and colour-coded the same as the check-list so that parents can easily find the card corresponding to the check-list item they are going to teach.

The activity cards are for recording the teaching activities which parents work on between visits from the Portage worker. The book of readings provides parents with a description of and a rationale for the teaching system used in the Portage programme.

Home visits by the Portage worker are normally weekly and are scheduled to last about one and a half hours. The child's progress on the item which parents have worked on over the week is checked by referring to the activity card and by getting the child to demonstrate the skill. If the child can now accomplish this task a tick is placed on the check-list and another item is selected to work on. If the child has not yet learnt the particular skill the Portage worker will discuss alternative teaching strategies with the parents.

The emphasis in the programme is on Portage workers establishing partnerships with parents with the aim of empowering them to facilitate the development of their children with special needs. Thus, the concept of professionals sharing their skills with parents is a key element of the programme. In practice, Portage workers find that allowing time on home visits for discussing parents' concerns about their children helps to promote this partnership. In slightly adapted forms the Portage model is now widely used in the UK (White and Cameron, 1988) and in over 30 countries throughout the world (Brouillette *et al.*, 1993).

PARENT BEHAVIOURAL TRAINING

The most radical approach to parental involvement in education has gained steadily in popularity since it emerged during the 1970s (Berkowitz and Graziano, 1972; Graziano and Diament, 1992). The aim of Parent Behavioural Training (PBT) is to teach parents the skills of behaviour modification so that they can work directly on their children's behaviour problems or learning difficulties. The idea is that parents act as their children's behaviour therapists or teachers either alone or in collaboration with professionals.

There are several components of the rationale for this approach:

(1) It is considered that parents are children's natural teachers since they teach them self-help and language skills in the pre-school years.
(2) Since parents spend so much time with their children they have ample opportunities for teaching them.
(3) Involving parents in this way should result in long-term gains for their children since parents will have learnt skills they can use throughout childhood.
(4) Training parents to act as therapists or teachers to their children, rather than professionals working with them directly, is more cost-effective in terms of professional time.

In the first years of PBT the emphasis was very much on remediating children's behaviour problems but subsequently children's learning difficulties have received more attention. For example, parents have been trained to act as therapists for children with delayed language (Topping, 1986). Also, the technology of PBT has progressed substantially since the early days. At first, PBT programmes relied solely on teaching parents how to positively reinforce appropriate behaviour. Then, when it was realized that this had limited effectiveness, the technique of extinction, or ignoring inappropriate behaviour, was added. Later, it was realized that successful training needed to include teaching parents effective methods of punishment such as withdrawal of privileges and time out. As sophistication in the techniques taught to parents for dealing with behaviour problems increased so did those for remediating learning difficulties. In addition, the methods used to train parents in these techniques became increasingly sophisticated. These aspects of PBT are discussed in detail in Topping (1986) and the main components are summarized below.

Training methods

The methods used to train parents in behavioural principles and techniques have included:

- lecture presentations
- video-taped modelling
- live modelling
- role play
- behavioural rehearsal
- feedback
- home visits
- telephone monitoring of progress
- parent self-recording
- parent training manuals.

Of the wide range of training methods noted above which have been used Graziano and Diament (1992) found that self-instructional materials, such as the parent training manuals written by Patterson (1975) and Newsome and Hipgrave (1982), could be successful and cost-effective. However, the most effective forms of PBT were found to be ones which included the active participation of parents, such as modelling and role play or feedback given on home visits.

Training content

The techniques taught to parents to deal with their children's *behaviour problems* have included:

- observation techniques
- methods of parent recording
- contingent attention (positive reinforcement)
- point incentive systems (star charts and token systems)
- extinction (ignoring)
- time out
- response cost (withdrawal of privileges)
- contingency contracting (for secondary school age children)
- fading (of extrinsic reinforcers back to natural consequences).

The techniques taught to parents in order that they can remediate their children's *learning difficulties* include:

- the effective use of rewards
- prompting
- cueing
- task analysis
- shaping
- backward chaining
- fading.

Graziano and Diament (1992) conclude from their recent review that PBT has been found to be effective in dealing with a wide range of children's behaviour problems and learning difficulties. Parents have been shown to benefit from PBT by improving their know-ledge of behavioural techniques and application of child manage-ment skills as well as in developing more positive attitudes to their children. Individual and group PBT were found to be equally effective which suggests that since group PBT is more cost-effective, this may generally be the preferred approach. Group behavioural training is discussed in Chapter 8.

PARENTAL INVOLVEMENT IN READING

A type of parental involvement in the education of children in mainstream primary and secondary schools which has gained considerably in popularity since the late 1970s involves parents helping their children with reading at home. Parent involvement with reading has taken a variety of forms, based on the different approaches or programmes which have been adopted by schools, as documented in Topping and Wolfendale (1985). Three of the most widely used types of programmes for promoting parental involvement in reading are parent listening, paired reading and the approach known as Pause, Prompt and Praise. These three approaches are outlined below.

Parent listening

Listening to children read the books they bring home from school is the time-honoured way for parents to help their children learn to read. It is a method now used in virtually all primary schools in one way or another. The effectiveness of this approach was affirmed by the study conducted by Tizard *et al.* (1982) which was referred to earlier in this chapter. The results of this study showed that when parents listened to their children read at home they made substan-tial gains in reading attainment. Furthermore, these gains were greater than those made by other children who had been given extra tuition in reading at school instead of being exposed to parent listening. In addition, a follow-up study has subsequently found that the gains which children in the parent listening group had made were maintained four years later (Hewison, 1985).

Another study which focused on parent listening was conducted in Belfield, a low SES suburb of Rochdale, about a mile from where I grew up (Hannon *et al.*, 1985). The aim of the project was to encourage as many parents as possible to hear their children read on a regular basis. Parents enrolled in the project when their children were aged 5 and many participated for two or three years. Meetings held at the school were used to explain the project to the parents. Later in the project these meetings included an introductory video. Carefully designed procedures were implemented to ensure that parents listened to their children read each night after school. Plastic folders were supplied so that books could be safely transported to and from school by the children. Record cards which parents filled in were used so that teachers could monitor parent listening and quickly identify any parents who needed help.

Considerable emphasis was placed on maintaining close working relationships with parents throughout their involvement in the project. Parents were all visited at home at least once during the first term that they became involved in the project. Meetings were held at school about the project at which lists of what to do and what not to do were handed out. In addition, letters were regularly sent home with the children and teachers attempted to speak to parents at every opportunity, such as when they were dropping off their children at school or picking them up. In fact, it was considered that a key factor in maintaining parents' interest in and co-operation with the project was the personal relationships which teachers established with parents.

Before the project began 38 per cent of parents reported that they listened to their children read almost daily. The mean reading quotient of the children whose parents listened to them read was found to be significantly higher than that of the remaining children, as found in other studies of parent listening. Interviews carried out with parents who had spent two years in the project found that 90 per cent of children were heard reading almost daily at home. This represents a substantial improvement in the level of parent involvement in their children's reading which, surprisingly, did not result in a significant improvement in overall levels of achievement in reading for the children involved (Hannon, 1987). However, it is possible that the project had a long-term impact on these children's progress due to raising their parents' awareness of the value of involving themselves in their children's education.

The two studies of parent listening described above provide a powerful rationale for the use of such schemes. One of the main advantages of this approach is its versatility. Parent listening can be used to support any approach to reading or reading scheme which schools use. Also, it requires minimal input of teacher time and other resources for what is an appreciable benefit. The main weakness of this approach is the uncertainty about 'how' parents listen to their children reading. What do they actually do? It is very likely that different parents will handle the sessions quite differently and it is possible that some parents may create problems through their lack of understanding of how children learn to read. For this reason the technique of 'paired reading', which is described in the next section, is generally regarded as a superior approach.

Paired reading

The main way in which paired reading differs from parent listening is that more guidance is provided on how parents should act when they are hearing children read. Parents are encouraged to use the procedure regularly for short periods. Children are allowed to select their own books for reading to their parents. The paired reading procedure has two phases. In the first phase the parent and child read together out loud with the parent adjusting to the child's pace of reading. When the child reads a word incorrectly the parent says the word correctly and gets the child to repeat the word before the two of them continue reading together.

In the second phase, when children feel confident enough to read alone, they signal to the parent to be silent, usually by a nudge from the elbow, and continue to read aloud by themselves. The parent then praises the child for taking this initiative and continues to praise the child's efforts when difficult words are mastered and when errors are spontaneously corrected by the child. When the child makes a mistake the parent says the word correctly, gets the child to repeat the word and then joins in reading out loud with the child as before. When the child gets stuck on a word the parent waits about four or five seconds and then supplies the word and gets the child to say it correctly before continuing to read aloud together. When children again feel confident they can once more signal to the parent to be silent and continue to read on by themselves.

Several variations of the paired reading procedure are reported in Topping and Wolfendale (1985). One variation is 'shared reading' which is regarded as a simplification of paired reading (Greening and Spenceley, 1984). Paired reading simply involves parents reading aloud with their children while ignoring any mistakes that they make. The aim of this approach is to increase the flow of reading and focus attention on to the meaning of the text. In another variation an additional phase is added to the paired reading procedure to cope with books of high interest to children but which are really too difficult for them. The first phase consists of parents reading a short passage aloud by themselves with children following the text. The second phase involves the parent and child reading the passage aloud together with parents either correcting mistakes or supplying words as described above. In the third phase children attempt to read the passage by themselves with parents correcting and praising as above (Bryans *et al.*, 1985).

In all paired reading approaches the key factors in ensuring effectiveness are how well parents are trained to carry out the procedures and the monitoring and support provided to ensure that parents correctly implement the procedures at home. Most paired reading projects begin by organizing a meeting of interested parents at school. This meeting is also often used to provide group training to parents in operating the procedures. Many LEAs have demonstration videotapes of the paired reading procedures available for schools to borrow to show parents. Alternatively, in some projects parents have been given brief individual training in carrying out paired reading (Bryans *et al.*, 1985). Record sheets for parents to fill in after each reading session are also used so that they provide a means of monitoring how parents and children are getting on.

Reviews of studies which have compared the effectiveness of parent listening, paired reading and other procedures in improving children's reading attainment have suggested that paired reading is generally the most effective approach (Topping, 1985; Topping and Lindsay, 1992). A recent study has found that a key element in the effectiveness of paired reading is that parents are able to maintain the flow of reading so that children's interest in and comprehension of what they are reading is enhanced (Elliott and Hewison, 1994). It is suggested that paired reading helps to shift the emphasis away from viewing reading as an exercise to be worked through to focusing on comprehension and enjoyment of the story.

However, Elliott and Hewison also reported that many parents complained that using this approach all the time was too limiting. They wanted to use additional strategies to help their children cope with words they found difficult. This is precisely the aim of the approach known as Pause, Prompt and Praise, which is described in the next section.

Pause, Prompt and Praise

The approach to parental involvement in reading called Pause, Prompt and Praise (PPP) was developed in New Zealand by Glynn (1985) and his colleagues. The emphasis in the PPP approach is on careful training of parents in a tutoring procedure which focuses on the meaning of the text and emphasizes the need to allow children time to 'self-correct' any errors they make. The PPP tutoring procedure includes the following aspects. First of all, it is important to ensure that children are given reading material of an appropriate level of difficulty, that is, text on which their reading accuracy is between 80 and 95 per cent. Below 80 per cent accuracy the material is too difficult, 95 per cent and above it is too easy. Therefore, parents are taught a simple way of checking difficulty level so that books of a suitable level can be selected for tutoring. Most often the PPP approach is used in conjunction with a reading scheme which includes a series of books graded into progressive difficulty levels. This facilitates the selection of books for parents and children to work on.

In the first step of the PPP tutoring procedure, when children make an error parents pause for a few seconds to allow children to attempt to correct it themselves. If this does not happen then parents offer prompts related to the type of error that is made. If the mistake does not make sense then the parent prompts with clues about the meaning of the story. If the mistake does make sense then the parent prompts with clues about how the word looks. When children do not attempt to say the word then they are told to read on to the end of the sentence, or to re-read the sentence from the beginning, in order to help them focus on contextual clues. If the incorrect word is not read correctly after two prompts the word is supplied. Praise is given for correct reading, self-correction and for correcting mistakes following prompts.

The research studies on PPP have typically involved individual training of parent tutors with twice-weekly sessions held in their homes (Glynn, 1985). Parents were given a diagrammatic summary of the PPP procedure and feedback was provided on actual tutoring sessions which they were observed conducting with their children and on other tutoring sessions which they recorded on audio tapes. In studies carried out in both Auckland and Birmingham very promising results were obtained with children whose attainments in reading were markedly delayed.

A booklet for parents explaining the procedure has been produced (Glynn *et al.*, 1979) and subsequently a trainer's manual and videotape demonstration of PPP have become available (McNaughton *et al.*, 1987). So it is now possible to set up projects using PPP involving less intensive methods such as group training of parent tutors, in the same way that this is done in paired reading and parent listening projects. In fact, Merrett (1988), in his review of the literature on the topic, suggests that parents can be taught the PPP procedures 'relatively quickly and easily and that their application is successful in bringing about important changes for the better in low-progress readers' (p. 22).

PARENTAL INVOLVEMENT IN OTHER CURRICULUM AREAS

Following the success of projects aimed at increasing parental involvement in reading this general approach has also begun to be focused on other areas of the school curriculum from basic academic skills such as spelling to more specific aspects such as European awareness. Topping (1986) describes parent involvement programmes which have focused on: perceptual training for nursery age children; spelling for primary school children; and mathematics for secondary school children. Wolfendale (1992) outlines projects which have focused on: language development; literacy skills; and numeracy. An excellent example of these programmes which have focused on curriculum areas other than reading are the multiply attainments through home support (MATHS) projects co-ordinated by Bamford and Arora (1988).

Bamford and Arora describe a series of projects aimed at involving parents in helping their children with mathematics using a games approach. All the projects were aimed at children in primary schools and followed a similar format. First, the project co-ordinators, who were educational psychologists, met with the headteacher and members of staff to decide on the children to be involved and the length of the project, which was usually six or eight weeks. Next, parents were invited to a meeting at the school at which the project was described and a booklet about the project given out. At the end of the meeting parents chose a mathematics game to take home to play with their children. Over 40 different games were used, all focusing on early mathematical concepts such as matching, shape and conservation. Accompanying each game was a card with a list of words to use while playing the game and on which parents recorded the amount of time spent playing the game. It was suggested that parents spend ten to fifteen minutes each day playing the game with their children over the following week. Parents then visited the school each week to exchange their games. At the end of the project parents were invited to the school to discuss their experiences and provide feedback to the organizers. Finally, they were given a booklet of mathematics games to take home.

The authors have attempted to evaluate the projects through feedback from parents and teachers involved and from observations of the children. They conclude that both parents and children enjoy playing the games and that children's confidence and enjoyment of mathematics increases following the project. They also suggest that the projects result in an increase in children's understanding of mathematical language and concepts.

FACILITATING PARENTAL INVOLVEMENT IN ASSESSMENTS AND REVIEWS

The importance of involving parents in the assessment of their children with special educational needs, and reviews of their progress, has recently been reinforced by the emphasis placed on this aspect of parental involvement in the *Code of Practice on the Identification and Assessment of Special Educational Needs* (DFE, 1994). Since parental involvement in assessments and reviews, including statutory assessments and annual reviews of statements, are now mandated by the Code of Practice schools will have to think very carefully about how they are going to involve parents who have children with special educational needs. In addition, as I have argued throughout this book, children with special needs of any kind, including those coping with medical conditions and losses through bereavement or divorce, also benefit from maximum involvement of their parents in their education. Therefore, facilitating optimum involvement of parents in assessments and reviews is considered important for children with all types of special needs.

In fact, Wolfendale (1992) suggests that assessments should ideally be conducted by means of a partnership between parents and teachers. In the early stages they should encompass the sharing of information with both parents and teachers setting out their opinions and concerns about children. Later, more specific data on the child's development can be collected by parents and teachers by such means as observations, check-lists and tests. The information collected is then shared in a parent–teacher meeting so that an assessment of the child's behaviour and attainments in both home and school settings is achieved. Viewing parental and teacher assessment data as complementary in this way leads to a more open sharing of concerns and ideas between the two and thereby promotes the development of a collaborative partnership.

What parents want from assessments

Many parents of children with special needs experience considerable anxiety about assessments conducted with their children. They realise the importance of the results of such assessments in making decisions about appropriate placements, about the amount of specialist help the child will receive and about the likely future development of the child. Most parents are therefore very keen to know about any assessments their children are to undergo and like to receive feedback on such assessments as soon as possible afterwards.

Wolfendale (1992) suggests that parents typically have five main expectations when their children are assessed. They want to know what steps will be taken as a result of the assessment and what they can do to help. They want to be able to discuss their children's past performance with their current teacher, and to hear constructive comments on their children's current rate of progress in relation to their previous achievements and to the performance of other children. They also want to know what strategies teachers are going to use in order to address their children's difficulties, and they seek confirmation that their children are happy and making progress in their current school.

Broadfoot (1989) reports some research which highlights key aspects of the information about assessments which parents want from teachers. Most importantly, it needs to be *objective*; information must be able to be substantiated rather than merely being based on speculation. Also, it needs to be *constructive*; teachers' comments must include strategies for improving progress. The information must also be *significant*; it should focus on important areas of the child's development. Ideally, the information should also be *succinct*; teachers' comments should be brief and to the point. It also needs to be *goal-related*; comments should be related to parents' goals for their children. Finally, such information must be *broadly-based*; it should focus on a broad view of their children's needs.

What parents can contribute to assessments

Wolfendale (1992) has summarized the research on parental contributions to assessments and concluded that 'the quality of content of parental input is equal to that of trained professionals . . .' (p. 79). She considers that parents can make an invaluable contribution to the assessment process for several reasons. First of all, parents have extensive knowledge of their children's development from birth onwards from which they can contribute comments about any specific difficulties they have experienced or particular assets which they have demonstrated. Parents also have an intimate knowledge of the family history and current circumstances which may be affecting the child. In addition, parents often have knowledge of other factors, related to the wider social environment in which the family lives, which can have an impact on the child. Parents can also supply knowledge of their children's behaviour in the home setting which may well be different to that at school. Furthermore, the information supplied by parents is considered to complement that from professionals and therefore can serve to highlight concerns regarding their children's progress. Finally, it is considered that parents are able to make realistic appraisals of their children and thereby make a significant contribution to the assessment process.

Increasing the effectiveness of parental involvement in assessments and reviews

It has been argued above that involving parents in the assessment and review processes is likely to significantly improve the quality of information available. It is therefore important to attempt to optimize the effectiveness of parental involvement in these processes. In the past, parents were often seen merely as recipients of information who were asked to comment on the assessment data produced by professionals. It is now considered that the effectiveness of assessments and reviews is substantially improved when parents are treated as active partners in the process of collecting and reviewing assessment data. However, most parents are unlikely to contribute optimally unless their involvement is actively sought by teachers. Strategies which can be used to increase parental involvement in assessments and reviews are discussed below.

Assessments Several examples of strategies used to improve the effectiveness of parental input into the assessment of children have been reported by Wolfendale (1993). These have involved the completion of diaries, observation charts, developmental checklists and parental profiles, by parents, in collaboration with teachers, in order to assess the behaviour and development of children. Parental profiles have been used in situations as diverse as assessing children's progress prior to their entry into school as rising 5-year-olds and preparing material to present as the parental advice required for statutory assessments.

There is now general recognition of the benefits of providing parents with pro formas to guide their input into the assessment process. The Code of Practice (DFE, 1994) provides guidelines to this effect. It therefore seems expedient to use these for all assessments conducted with children who have special needs. Clearly different pro formas will need to be used for children of different ages and to suit the particular situation for which they are to be used. However, most pro formas will seek information from parents about the following:

- child's health, especially any medication taken or known medical problems
- gross motor skills, such as walking, jumping and throwing
- fine motor skills, such as drawing, handwriting and assembling small objects

- self-help skills, such as dressing, toileting and travelling independently
- communication skills, such as clarity of speech, vocabulary and length of sentences
- basic academic skills, such as reading, writing, spelling and number skills
- work habits, such as concentration span and study skills
- play/leisure skills, such as hobbies and sporting activities
- behaviour outside school, such as in the home or on family outings
- relationships, such as with parents, siblings, other family members and friends.

Reviews Pro formas for parents to complete beforehand can also be used to improve parents' participation in reviews of their children's progress. An example of this is provided by Hughes and Carpenter (1991) who describe the development and use of a Parents' Comments Form (PCF), which is intended to help parents organize their thoughts on their child's progress and needs so that they can contribute more meaningfully to the annual reviews of the child's statement of special educational needs. In an evaluation of the use of the PCF, with parents of children attending a special school for children with severe learning difficulties, it was reported that parents found the forms helpful in preparing for the review meetings and it was considered that this led to a more effective partnership between parents and teachers. Clearly, pro formas which parents can use to provide information on their children as part of a review of their progress will need to be designed to take children's ages and special needs into account. However, most pro formas will seek comments from parents about changes in the following areas since the previous review:

- child's health, for example, any significant illnesses, changes in medication or diet
- behaviour, any significant problems either in the home or outside it
- abilities, any significant difficulties or progress made
- likes and dislikes, current likes and dislikes which the child expresses
- independence, any significant progress toward independence
- priority areas, any weaknesses which need to be overcome or strengths to develop
- home circumstances, anything which may be affecting the child's behaviour at school.

SUMMARY AND CONCLUSIONS

Reviews of the literature and personal experience have provided convincing evidence of the effectiveness of parental involvement in promoting children's education. The origins of parent involvement have been traced to early intervention programmes such as Project High/Scope and the Portage project whose use continues to increase in popularity throughout the world. Another area of children's education in which parents have been involved long term is reading. Three approaches to parent involvement in reading are described: parent listening; paired reading; and Pause, Prompt and Praise. Behavioural training of parents is another aspect of parent involvement which has a fairly long history. Its focus on reducing behaviour problems and remediating children's learning difficulties are described. More recent, in this country, has been the involvement of parents in assessments of children and reviews of their progress. What parents want out of assessments and can contribute to them is discussed and strategies for improving parental input into the assessment and review processes are described.

8

Working with parents in groups

INTRODUCTION

I became involved in group work with parents quite by chance. When, as a trainee educational psychologist in New Zealand, I noticed that there were six referrals from parents whose children attended the same large primary school, all wanting guidance on managing their children's behaviour, I decided to see them in a group. I did this mainly to save time, but as the sessions progressed it became clear that parents were finding it very useful to be able to discuss their problems within the group and, as a result, I became more and more convinced of the value of the group approach in helping parents.

Then a friend, who was a teacher at a special school for children with severe learning difficulties, suggested that the parents there would also benefit from group work which focused on managing their children's behaviour. I then began to team up with colleagues in order to run groups for parents of children with severe learning difficulties at several special schools in Auckland (Hornby, 1980). This led naturally to providing group programmes for parents of children with other disabilities such as hearing impairment and physical disability (Hornby and Murray, 1983).

In leading these workshops it became clear that, although parents benefited from the professional input, they appeared to gain at least equally from talking with other parents in similar situations to themselves. So when I heard about Parent to Parent schemes at a special education conference in Perth, Western Australia, in 1982, my colleagues and I decided to set up a pilot scheme in Auckland (Hornby *et al.*, 1987). Parent to Parent services involve training parents in groups so that they can provide support to other parents who have children with special needs. Parent to Parent schemes have now been set up in all major cities in New Zealand and, after ten years of operation, they have a national organization which includes an annual conference. In the last few years Parent to Parent schemes have also begun to be set up in the UK (Hornby, 1988).

The benefits to parents of workshops and self-help groups such as Parent to Parent have convinced me of the importance of group experiences in providing support and guidance to parents who have children with special needs. The aim of this chapter is, therefore, to describe various types of group work with parents and discuss key aspects such as leadership skills and group process variables so that teachers, in collaboration with other professionals, can provide such experiences for parents. The chapter also includes a discussion of the specific benefits of working with groups of parents. In addition, brief descriptions of the organization of parent workshops and Parent to Parent schemes are presented.

BENEFITS OF GROUP WORK WITH PARENTS

Probably the most important benefit of working with groups of parents is that, in talking with others, parents realize that they are not the only ones with problems. This sharing of common problems typically leads to parents feeling that they are all 'in the same boat' which is a particularly therapeutic component of group work (Yalom, 1985). In addition, parents can express their feelings regarding their children with special needs and discover that others have similar feelings, which often helps them come to terms with their own. Further, in a group with other parents of children with special needs it is often easier for parents to reveal concerns which they have not felt able to bring up individually.

Another benefit of group work is that parents experience mutual support from the other group members which helps them to become more confident in their own ability as parents. The group also provides the opportunity to practise communication skills such as the expression of feelings and the ability to listen empathically to others (Dinkmeyer and Muro, 1979). A further benefit of group work is that when parents participate in a group they learn together in a mutually supportive atmosphere. They are often more responsive to changing their opinions and learning new strategies in this situation (Kroth, 1985). Also, in a group, parents are exposed to a wider range of behaviour problems and learning difficulties, and the techniques used to deal with them, which may facilitate their handling of similar problems encountered in the future.

Another benefit is that, in a group, solutions for a particular parent's difficulties will be suggested by other parents who may have experienced similar difficulties in the past. Parents are almost always responsive to such potential solutions. Groups also provide numerous possibilities for modelling and role play of difficult situations, and are a source of ideas for potential reinforcers, motivation, and social reinforcement (Rose, 1977).

There are also advantages of working with groups of parents for the professionals involved. Obviously, since more parents can be reached in a group than individually it is possible to help a greater number of parents than could be managed using an individual approach. Also, there are times when several parents are experiencing the same difficulty and teachers can provide guidance to them all at the same time rather than individually, thereby using their time more efficiently. Another advantage is that, because of the efficient use of time in group work, it is possible to justify two or more professionals working together with the group of parents and thereby sharing skills and knowledge with each other. Working with colleagues such as teachers, psychologists, speech therapists, occupational therapists and social workers in groups has contributed significantly to my expertise in working with parents. In addition, the parents in the group are a source of knowledge and skills which professionals can utilize. Working with parent groups is a powerful way to educate teachers about parents' experiences and needs.

However, there are some costs of doing group work with parents of children with special needs. Some parents do not feel comfortable being in a group with other parents and prefer to be seen individually. Also, in order to obtain maximum participation in group work with parents it is often necessary to hold sessions in evenings or at the weekend, which can cut into teachers' leisure and preparation time. Finally, working with groups of parents requires skills and knowledge over and above that needed for individual work, so these need to be acquired to a reasonable level before embarking on group work with parents (Seligman, 1990). Group leadership skills and knowledge of group dynamics are discussed next.

GROUP LEADERSHIP SKILLS AND KNOWLEDGE

The skills needed to lead group work with parents of children with special needs include those which were discussed in Chapter 5, that is, counselling skills, assertion skills and most importantly listening skills. However, the skills required in order to lead such groups are more comprehensive than those needed for individual work with parents. Dinkmeyer and Muro (1979) agree that, first and foremost, group leaders need to be skilled listeners. They suggest that leaders also need to be able to develop trust within the group and to maintain a focus on the goals both of the group as a whole and of the individuals within it. Further, that leaders need to be spontaneous and to be responsive to what is happening within the group at any point in time. They need to be able to combine the ability to stand firm with a good sense of humour. Finally, to be effective, they need to be perceived by group members as being with them as a group and for them as individuals.

Another perspective on leadership skills which I have found particularly useful is that provided by Trotzer (1977) who considers that group leaders need the skills of reaction, interaction and action. These are briefly outlined below.

The reaction skills which leaders need are:

- listening, in order to communicate respect, acceptance, empathy and caring
- restating, to convey to group members that they are being heard
- reflecting, to convey understanding and help members to express themselves
- clarifying, to better understand confusing aspects of what is said
- summarizing, to provide an overview, stimulate reactions and move on to new ground.

The interaction skills which leaders need are:

- moderating, to ensure that all group members have the opportunity to talk
- interpreting, to help members gain insight into what is happening within the group
- linking, to tie together common elements within the group and promote cohesiveness
- blocking, to prevent undesirable action by one or more group members
- supporting, to encourage members to share of themselves safely within the group
- limiting, to prevent actions which would infringe the rights of group members
- protecting, to prevent group members from being unduly criticized or hurt
- consensus-taking, to help members see where they stand in relation to others.

The action skills which leaders need are:

- questioning, to help members consider aspects they had not thought of
- probing, to help members look more deeply into their concerns
- tone-setting, to establish an atmosphere and qualitative standard to be adhered to

- confronting, to help members face things about themselves which they are avoiding
- personal sharing, to show that the leader is human and is prepared to open up
- modelling, to teach members interpersonal skills such as active listening.

Group dynamics

In addition to these skills, leaders also need to have a good understanding of group dynamics, that is, the processes which occur within groups. There are several models of the process of group development and each suggests that all groups need to pass through several stages or phases if they are to function well and achieve their goals. The various models differ in the number of stages included and in some of the characteristics of the stages but there is considerable overlap (for example see Corey, 1990; Trotzer, 1977). The one which I have found most useful in understanding what happens in groups is that proposed by Williamson (1982), which has four stages: inclusion; work; action; and termination. These are outlined below.

Inclusion The first stage of any group is one of developing a group cohesiveness so that all members feel a part of the group. Particip-ants need to feel comfortable about belonging to the group. They need to be willing to share aspects of themselves and to explore concerns and issues within the group. Some time will be needed for this to develop as members tentatively interact with the leader and each other. As this process develops, group norms or implicit group rules will begin to be established.

Work The second stage is one in which the members begin to work on resolving the concerns or issues related to the purpose of the group. This is usually the longest stage in the group's life. It involves members in discussing ideas, expressing feelings and listening to others in order to gain insight into their own situation. It is in this stage that group members will experience the greatest benefit. However, some members will resist change and there will be conflict and tension within the group. At the same time relation-ships between other group members will deepen and become more meaningful. The work stage can be regarded as providing a transi-tion between members becoming part of the group and deciding what action to take.

Action In the third stage, the understanding and growth which occurs in the work stage needs to be translated into some form of action, otherwise the group will not fulfil its purpose. Individual members, or the group as a whole, need to decide what action to take to address the concerns which brought them into the group. Since change is difficult for members to cope with the group needs to provide them with considerable support during this stage.

Termination The final stage is one in which the group comes to a close with members experiencing a sense of completion, accomplishment and gratitude for what the group has helped them achieve.

When groups progress through these four stages then the experience can be a very powerful one in promoting learning and personal growth in the members. I have observed this happen on numerous occasions with parents of children with special needs who have participated in the parent workshops or Parent to Parent training courses discussed later in this chapter. The growth in confidence of many parents over the period of these projects has often been startling. Unfortunately, however, because groups can be so powerful, when they are badly led they can result in members having their self-confidence reduced, as I have experienced myself. So it is essential to ensure that qualified and experienced leaders are employed for any group work carried out with parents.

PARENT EDUCATION GROUPS

Since the 1970s interest in attending courses in parent education from parents in general has grown steadily in the USA but has been much slower to develop in the UK. Several programmes for group parent education using substantially different approaches have been developed and disseminated. The approaches described in this section are Parent Effectiveness Training, Parent Behavioural Training and some other less widely used programmes.

Parent Effectiveness Training

Parent Effectiveness Training (PET) is the most widely disseminated parent education programme in the Western world with hundreds of thousands of parents having participated in it. It is based on the book of the same name which became an international bestseller for the author, Thomas Gordon (1970). The aim of the programme is to facilitate communication and improve relationships between parents and their children. The programme consists of an eight-week course attended by ten to twelve parents with a leader who has been trained in leading PET groups. The methods used by leaders are a combination of demonstration and role play of the skills being taught with open discussions conducted in a circle.

The programme focuses on four key aspects of parent–child relationships.

(1) Parents are taught listening skills so that they can improve their ability to listen to their children. The most essential aspect of this is learning active listening, the skill which was discussed in Chapter 5.

(2) Parents are taught how to express their feelings using 'I' messages in order to avoid using 'you' messages which tend to put the blame on their children.

(3) Parents are taught how to analyse ownership of a problem so that they can decide which are their problems and which should be left with the child. The importance of allowing children to accept ownership of problems which belong to them is emphasized.

(4) For problems whose ownership lies with both parents and children parents are taught how to use a six-step method for resolving the conflict which is called 'no-lose problem solving'.

There are numerous positive reports of the effectiveness of PET in improving parents' relationships with their children but the results of reviews of the more rigorous studies are less convincing (Rinn and Markle, 1977).

Other forms of parent education

There are several other forms of group parent education programmes which have been designed for parents in general. Two of the better known of these will now be briefly described in order to demonstrate the wide range of approaches which are available. Systematic Training for Effective Parenting (STEP) is a programme based on the ideas of Alfred Adler (1927) which have been developed into a parent education kit by Dinkmeyer and McKay (1976). The aim of STEP is to help parents develop a better understanding of their children's behaviour, improve communication with them and increase parents' influence over their children's behaviour. The STEP kit includes a leader's manual; charts which illustrate the main concepts to be taught; group discussion guideline cards; and cassette tapes with brief lectures and skill-building exercises for parents. Key aspects of the programme are study of the goals of children's behaviour and the application of natural consequences to deal with misbehaviour.

The Transactional Analysis (TA) approach to parent education is based on the ideas of Berne (1964) and Harris (1969) which have been applied to children by Babcock and Keepers (1976). The aims of group parent education based on this approach are to increase parents' understanding of their relationships with their children and thereby to improve communication within the family. Key concepts in this approach are the 'ego states' of parent, adult and child which are highlighted in family communication and the complementary, crossed and ulterior transactions which occur within families. Also important are the 'basic life positions' adopted by individuals and the unconscious 'games' played by family members. Sessions include both didactic and experiential components. Relevant reading and practical homework assignments are used and specific problems brought to the group by participants are discussed and brainstormed within the group.

No research evaluations of either STEP or the TA approach to parent education could be found in the literature so it must be assumed that although these are promising approaches their effectiveness in improving parent–child relationships has not been demonstrated.

Behavioural group training

Behavioural Group Training (BGT) is an extension of the principles of Parent Behavioural Training (discussed in Chapter 7) to work with groups of parents. It is a widely used approach to parent education with parents of children with behavioural problems and other kinds of special needs. The aim of BGT is to teach parents the principles and practice of behavioural analysis in order to improve their management of their children's behavioural and learning difficulties. BGT typically consists of an eight- to ten-week course attended by six to twelve parents and led by psychologists trained in behavioural methods. The training techniques used by the leaders include: lectures; modelling; role play; parent training manuals; discussion; and homework assignments.

BGT programmes typically include the concept of positive reinforcement of appropriate behaviour, as well as discussion of the different types of reinforcers which parents can use and conditions for their effective use. Also covered are other techniques used to increase levels of appropriate behaviour such as stimulus control, contingency contracting and Premack's Principle. In addition, techniques used to decrease levels of inappropriate behaviour are taught such as differential reinforcement, extinction, time out, response cost and over-correction. Finally, most programmes aimed at parents of children with special needs also include techniques used to develop new skills such as task analysis, shaping and backward chaining.

Research conducted to evaluate the effectiveness of BGT has presented some evidence to support the suggestion that parents do learn behavioural principles and techniques and are able to apply these with their children (Graziano and Diament, 1992; Hornby and Singh, 1983, 1984).

Comparative effectiveness of the different approaches

In a review of the field of parent education Tavormina (1974) found that most approaches could be classified as either reflective or behavioural. In reflective parent education programmes, such as Parent Effectiveness Training, the focus is on the parents' emotional needs. Parents are encouraged to discuss their concerns and opinions and express their feelings about their children. The aim is to help parents to understand and come to terms with the parenting role and thereby improve their ability to relate to their children. In behaviourally based parent education programmes, such as Group Behavioural Training, the focus is on teaching parents skills. Parents are taught behaviour modification techniques in order to facilitate the management of their children's behaviour and thereby improve parent–child relationships.

In a landmark study which compared the effectiveness of these two approaches with parents of children with special needs, Tavormina (1975) reported positive outcomes for both reflective and behavioural groups. In a further study it was found that a combination of reflective and behavioural approaches was the most effective (Tavormina *et al.*, 1976).

Group work with parents of children with special needs has generally taken the form of either reflective counselling (Hornby and Singh, 1982) or behavioural training (Hornby and Singh, 1983). However, positive outcomes have been widely reported when aspects of the reflective and behavioural approaches have been combined in workshops for parents of children with special educational needs (Attwood, 1978, 1979; Cunningham and Jeffree, 1975; Hornby, 1992). This form of parent education programme is described next.

WORKSHOPS FOR PARENTS OF CHILDREN WITH SPECIAL NEEDS

A model for a parent workshop which combines aspects of both reflective and behavioural approaches was developed by me and my colleagues in New Zealand (Hornby, 1987). The aim of this project was to develop a type of parent workshop which combines group guidance in the form of brief lectures with group counselling conducted by means of small group discussions. It was considered that this format would provide a supportive environment in which parents could learn new skills and gain confidence through talking with other parents. The workshop has been used with groups of parents of children with a wide variety of types of special needs (Hornby and Murray, 1983). Details of the parent workshop are presented below so that teachers can adapt it to suit the population of parents with whom they work.

Organization of workshops

The structure and organization of the workshop model presented here is based on previous work with parents of children with disabilities but the model can easily be adapted to suit parents of children with the wide range of special needs discussed in this book. A summary of the main aspects of workshop organization is presented below.

Recruitment The best method of recruitment of parents for workshops is by sending a letter of invitation to all parents of children with the special need being addressed who are attending the school. No form of selection has been found necessary in the past as parents for whom workshops are not suitable have tended not to participate from their own choice.

Venue A venue which is familiar to the parents, comfortable and easy to get to is best. School staffrooms are a popular choice of venue for smaller workshops.

Sessions Between six and eight weekly two-hour evening sessions have been found to be the most satisfactory. Less than six sessions is too few for parents to benefit from the therapeutic process which the group will experience as the workshop progresses. More than eight sessions is often too great a commitment of time and too tiring for parents and teachers alike. Anything greater than a one-week break between sessions, such as fortnightly or monthly sessions, leads to a considerable drop in attendance and therefore should be

avoided. Evening sessions are generally easier for both professionals and parents to attend. Two hours is considered to be the
optimum time for the length of sessions. Any less leaves insufficient
time for both discussion and lecture presentation.

Number of parents A reasonably large number of parents can be
catered for by taking the group of parents as a whole during the
lecture presentations, introduction and final summary sections of
the workshop and dividing them into small groups during the
discussion section. The size of the small groups needs to be large
enough to give a reasonable range of children and problems but
small enough to provide sufficient time for each parent to discuss
his or her concern. About six to ten parents is generally the most
satisfactory size.

Group leaders Small group discussions need to be led by professionals with previous experience of leading such groups. Teachers
with no experience can be involved as co-leaders who work in
tandem with the leader. In this way teachers can be trained to lead
their own groups in subsequent parent workshops.

Format of workshops

Workshops are typically divided into four parts: introduction;
lecture presentation; small group discussion; and summary. These
are outlined next.

Introduction The first 15 minutes of workshops are used to help
parents relax since many of them experience anxiety when they first
come along to group sessions where they are expected to talk about
their children. It provides an opportunity for parents to get to know
other parents and teachers informally and also overcomes the
problem of late arrivals interrupting the lecture presentations.

Lecture presentations Lectures of a maximum of 20 minutes in length
are presented to the whole group of parents, who are usually seated
in a horseshoe arrangement around the speaker. The topics of
the lectures are best determined by sending out a list of potential
topics beforehand and asking parents to choose. Where necessary,
relevant specialists can then be invited in to give some of the
lectures. Clearly the lecture topics will depend on the types of
special needs and the ages of the children whose parents are

involved in the workshops. For example, lecture topics used in workshops for parents of children with disabilities have included: speech and language development; behaviour management; social and emotional development; sexual development; services available; recreational activities; and vocational placement.

Small group discussions The largest block of time in the workshop, at least an hour, is given over to discussion which is conducted in small groups. Discussions are conducted in separate rooms, with chairs arranged in a circle. Groups usually consist of a leader, a co-leader and six to ten parents. Leaders guide the discussions using the skills mentioned earlier in this chapter.

Co-leaders work in tandem with leaders by focusing on the group dynamics and on the body language of group members so that they can draw the leader's attention to a parent who may want to say something but hasn't been noticed. Leaders and co-leaders should meet for half an hour before each session to plan the session and for a short time afterwards in order to debrief and discuss the subsequent sessions.

Summary With all the parents present a leader or co-leader from each small group reports back on the issues and concerns discussed in their group. Any hand-outs, such as a summary of the lecture content for that session, are distributed and homework tasks, such as the completion of behaviour observation forms, are explained.

It is important to conclude the formal aspects of each session punctually since many parents will have arranged babysitters and need to be home promptly. However, it has been found that some parents will remain to talk with other parents or professionals for up to half an hour afterwards.

PARENT TO PARENT SCHEMES

Another type of parent group which has shown rapid growth in numbers in recent years are Parent to Parent schemes. Parent to Parent schemes are support services for parents of children with special needs in which support is provided by a team of volunteer parents who themselves have children with special needs (Hornby, 1988; McConkey, 1985). Up to this time most schemes have been organized for parents of children with disabilities but the Parent to Parent model described here is applicable to parents of children with a wide range of special needs.

Typically, Parent to Parent services operate as a telephone contact helpline. Schemes are advertised by means of leaflets, posters or cards put on notice-boards in places where parents are likely to see them, such as libraries, health centres and schools. Parents seeking contact ring the helpline telephone number and are put in touch with a support parent who has a child with similar special needs.

The Parent to Parent schemes in which I and my colleagues have been involved have emphasized training parents in basic counselling skills, using the model presented in Chapter 5, since we regard this as essential if support parents are to provide an effective service (Hornby *et al.*, 1987). By training parents to help others, professionals are assisting the development of a support network which will meet many of the parents' needs. In this way the scheme can provide a type of assistance which makes use of the special contribution which only people who have been through similar experiences can offer (Hatch and Hinton, 1986) and which is complementary to the professional help available.

Recruiting support parents

Potential support parents are initially recruited by means of contact with existing parent groups and other organizations such as MENCAP or CRUSE. A maximum of 14 parents can attend each course. It is explained to these parents that they must attend at least seven out of eight sessions and attain an adequate level of counselling skills in order to become support parents.

Training course

The Parent to Parent training course is typically conducted in a series of eight weekly sessions of two hours each but it can also be held over two or three full days, usually at the weekend. The first two sessions of the training course focus on the sharing of parents' own experiences regarding their children with special needs. In the first session parents introduce themselves and talk about their families, in particular the child with special needs. The stage model of adaptation to loss, which was discussed in Chapter 3, is presented in the second session in order to encourage parents to explore their feelings about their children with special needs. In the next five sessions parents are taught basic counselling skills using the three-stage model of helping discussed in Chapter 5. Emphasis is placed on the development of active listening skills, as these are seen as the key to effective operation as a support parent. The final session focuses on the organization of a Parent to Parent scheme, including such issues as the distribution of publicity materials and the planning of a duty roster for telephone duties.

Leaders

In order to lead Parent to Parent training courses professionals need experience of leading groups, knowledge of the special needs concerned and an ability to teach basic counselling skills to adults. Since courses are usually tutored by two leaders, it is possible for these requirements to be shared between the co-leaders. The teaching techniques used in the course include: mini-lectures, discussions, modelling, practice of the skills in threesomes, homework and rounds, in which all the parents in turn are asked to say what they think or feel. The specific procedures used are described in detail in the Leaders' Training Manual (Hornby *et al.*, 1993).

Organization of the scheme

The detail of the organizational structure of each Parent to Parent scheme is best determined by the support parents with only general guidance from the professionals involved in the training. Typically, a number of parents who have completed the first training course form a steering committee in order to set up the mechanics of the scheme. In order to spread the load, and ensure involvement of as many parents as possible, committee members are encouraged to share out the various administrative tasks involved in running the service including: finance, publicity, liaison, the telephone system and training (see Hornby *et al.*, 1987, for details).

The schemes require minimal funding and usually facilitate the development of useful parent–professional partnerships. They can contribute significantly to the support networks which are available to parents of children with special needs. Other benefits which accrue from the schemes include the personal growth which parents typically make in completing the training course and the mutual support which develops among course members.

OTHER TYPES OF GROUP WORK

Workshops have been developed in order to address the needs of other members of families who have children with special needs, that is siblings, fathers, and grandparents. In addition, self-help groups and advocacy groups provide other sources of support for families who have children with special needs. All involve some form of group work and are outlined below.

Grandparent workshops

Workshops for grandparents are generally held on Saturdays and include either a guest speaker invited to address matters of concern to grandparents or a panel of parents or siblings to talk about their experiences. Time is also scheduled for grandparents to meet in small groups, facilitated by a professional, to share their concerns and feelings. The workshops can therefore provide opportunities for grandparents to meet each other as well as to obtain information from professionals about their grandchildren's special needs and guidance on how best to provide support for the family (Vadasy *et al.*, 1986).

A related development is the Helping Grandparent Programme in which experienced grandparents are trained in order to provide support to grandparents of newly diagnosed children (Sonnek, 1986). This scheme is based on the Parent to Parent model which was described earlier in this chapter.

Fathers' programmes

Fathers' programmes generally use a workshop format, meeting, for example, every two weeks on Saturday mornings (Meyer *et al.*, 1985). There are typically three components to fathers' programmes, the first two of which are similar to those in workshops for parents and grandparents. First, guest speakers provide fathers with information about their children's special needs and the services available. Second, discussion groups are used to enable fathers to discuss their concerns and interests with other fathers and thereby obtain peer support. Third, fathers bring their children along to the meetings so that part of the time allocated can be used for all the fathers and children to get together and take part in group activities or individual play. The aims of this component of fathers' programmes are both to encourage fathers to interact more with their children and to provide their wives with some respite from child-care responsibilities (Vadasy *et al.*, 1985).

Sibling workshops

Sibling workshops are aimed at providing siblings of children with special needs an opportunity to meet others in the same situation, to gain specific information on special needs, and to learn how to handle common incidents which occur in families which have a member with a special need of some kind (Meyer *et al.*, 1985b). Sibling workshops have followed a similar format to the workshops described above but have also included outings and activities aimed at providing enjoyment for the siblings themselves. In order to help the younger children open up about their worries and feelings some different activities have been included. For example, siblings are asked to write down their problems on paper which is put in a box and is later taken out and read out to everyone and discussed in the group, without identifying the writer.

Self-help groups

A major growth area in mental health services in recent years has been the proliferation of self-help groups, well known examples of which are Alcoholics Anonymous and Weight Watchers (Gitterman and Shulman,1986). Groups for parents of children with special needs have been no exception. In most cities around the world there are now self-help groups for parents of children with most types of special needs. These range from groups in which a small number of parents get together regularly for support to others which have become national organizations such as MENCAP and CRUSE.

Many of the therapeutic factors associated with group work, referred to earlier in this chapter, also work to promote personal growth in self-help groups. In such groups parents develop their own personal coping strategies and increase their social support networks.

Advocacy groups

A type of group training for parents which has emerged recently is programmes for training parents in advocacy skills (Schilling, 1988). The aim of advocacy training is to help parents to become advocates for their own children in order to obtain the best possible services for them and ultimately to become advocates for people with special needs in general. Advocacy training involves gaining information about the rights of children with special needs and about how to access the resources and services available to them. It also involves parents learning the assertion skills, which were discussed in Chapter 5, so that they can overcome any lack of confidence and advocate for their children assertively rather than aggressively.

Advocacy training programmes therefore typically consist of a combination of professional input and parental sharing about available resources and how to access them, plus the teaching of assertion skills through didactic presentations, along with modelling and role play of the relevant strategies. In these ways professionals are able to pass on to parents the knowledge and skills they need, thereby empowering parents to become as effective as possible in their task of caring for their children with special needs.

SUMMARY AND CONCLUSIONS

In this chapter it has been proposed that there are substantial benefits to parents of children with special needs from participating in various types of group work. The group leadership skills and knowledge of the process of group development needed in order to lead group work with parents were discussed. Various forms of parent education are described including Parent Effectiveness Training and Group Behavioural Training. Two forms of group work which are considered to be particularly useful to parents of children with special needs are parent workshops and Parent to Parent schemes. These have been described in some detail followed by brief descriptions of other forms of groups such as sibling workshops, fathers' programmes and self-help groups.

9

Working with parents: the future

Three recent trends have made it imperative for all teachers, not just those in special schools but teachers in ordinary primary and secondary schools, to develop effective working relationships with parents of children with special needs:

(1) The policy of inclusion of as many children with special educational needs as possible into ordinary schools is likely to continue in the foreseeable future. This means that teachers in mainstream schools are likely to have increased contact with such children and their parents.

(2) There is increasing recognition that children can have special needs resulting from a wide range of difficulties and circumstances. Besides the long-term special needs resulting from disabilities such as visual impairment and learning difficulties there are perhaps more temporary, special needs associated with children such as those who have remediable speech difficulties, or medical conditions, or who are suffering the consequences of traumatic situations such as a death in the family or divorce of their parents.

(3) Increased parental rights have been provided in recent Education Acts for parents in general, and in the 1993 Education Act and the *Code of Practice on the Identification and Assessment of Special Educational Needs* (DFE, 1994) for parents of children with special needs in particular. These increased rights will necessarily lead to increased interaction between parents and teachers, especially those in mainstream primary and secondary schools.

This book has provided a rationale for developing collaborative working relationships with parents of children with special needs. The effects of various types of special needs on parents and families has been described and the teacher's role in providing help to parents has been considered. A model which schools can use to help them develop their policy and practice of parent involvement has been presented and some key elements of implementing such policies have been discussed in detail, including communication strategies, methods of parent involvement, group work approaches and the interpersonal skills needed by teachers in order to work effectively with parents.

It is intended that this book will be used by practising teachers to improve their practice with parents of children with special needs. It is further hoped that teachers who have read the book will be able to influence the policy and practice of their school, and those of their colleagues, with regard to parent involvement.

In a survey jointly conducted by the author (Hornby *et al.*, 1991) it was found that the development of effective working relationships with parents of children with special needs was rated by senior professionals in the field of special education to be of similar importance to the development of specialized skills for teaching such children. It is therefore surprising that there is such a lack of emphasis on working with parents in both the initial training of teachers and in-service training for teachers in general, and for teachers of children with special educational needs in particular.

The lack of training for teachers in the skills and knowledge required for working effectively with parents is a situation which needs to be urgently addressed if the increased parental involvement required by recent legislation is to be effectively implemented. In fact, training in parental involvement needs to be built in to the professional preparation of all teachers, therapists, social workers, psychologists, medical personnel and other professionals who work with children with special needs (Hornby and Murray, 1987).

In initial teacher training there should be input on the importance of home–school relationships, on useful strategies for communication with parents, and on training in a basic level of interpersonal skills necessary for interacting with parents. In-service training courses for teachers who, for example, are acting as Special Educational Needs Co-ordinators in schools, should include input on the needs of parents of children with different types of special needs, the policy and practice of parent involvement, communication strategies, and group approaches to working with parents, along with advanced training in interpersonal skills (Hornby, 1990). It is hoped that this book will be helpful in fulfilling these initial and in-service training needs.

Bibliography

Adler, A. (1927) *Understanding Human Nature*. Greenwich, CT: Fawcett.

Allan, J. (1988) *Inscapes of the Child's World: Jungian Counseling in Schools and Clinics*. Dallas, TX: Spring.

Allan, J. and Bertoia, J. (1992) *Written Paths to Healing: Education and Jungian Child Counseling*. Dallas, TX: Spring.

Allan, J. and Nairne, J. (1984) *Class Discussions for Teachers and Counsellors in the Elementary School*. Toronto: University of Toronto Press.

Atkeson, K.M. and Forehand, R. (1979) Home-based reinforcement programmes designed to modify classroom behaviour: a review and methodological evaluation. *Psychological Bulletin* **86**, 1298–1308.

Atkin, J., Bastiani, J. and Goode, J. (1988) *Listening to Parents: An Approach to the Improvement of Home–School Relations*. London: Croom Helm.

Attwood, T. (1978) The Croydon workshop for parents of preschool mentally handicapped children. *Child: Care, Health and Development* **4**, 79–97.

Attwood, T. (1979) The Croydon workshop for parents of severely handicapped school-age children. *Child: Care, Health and Development* **5**, 177–88.

Babcock, D.E. and Keepers, T.D. (1976) *Raising Kids O.K.* New York: Grove.

Bamford, J. and Arora, T. (1988) M.A.T.H.S. – Multiply attainments through home support: progress and development. *Educational and Child Psychology*, **5**, (4), 48–53.

Bastiani, J. (ed.) (1987) *Parents and Teachers 1: Perspectives on Home–School Relations*. Windsor: NFER-Nelson.

Bastiani, J. (ed.) (1988) *Parents and Teachers 2: From Policy to Practice*. Windsor: NFER-Nelson.

Bastiani, J. (1989) *Working with Parents: A Whole School Approach*. Windsor: NFER-Nelson.

Batshaw, M.L., Perret, Y.M. and Carter, W.P. (1992) *Children with Disabilities: A Medical Primer* (3rd edn). Baltimore: Paul H. Brookes.

Bell, R.Q. (1968) A reinterpretation of the direction of effects in studies of socialization. *Psychological Review* **75** (2), 81–95.

Berger, M. and Foster, M. (1986) 'Applications of family therapy theory to research and interventions with families with mentally retarded children'. In Gallagher, J.J. and Vietze, P.M. (eds) *Families of Handicapped Persons: Research, Programs and Policy Issues*. Baltimore: Paul H. Brookes, pp. 251–60.

Berkowitz, B.P. and Graziano, A.M. (1972) Training parents as behavior therapists: a review. *Behavior Research and Therapy* **10**, 297–317.

Berne, E. (1964) *Games People Play*. New York: Grove.

Berrueta-Clement, J., Schweinhart, L., Barnett, W., Epstein, A. and Weikart, D. (1984) *Changed Lives: The Effects of the Perry Preschool Project on Youths Through Age 19*. Ypsilanti, MI: High Scope Press.

Bicknell, J. (1988) 'The psychopathology of handicap'. In Horobin, G. and May, D. (eds) *Living with Mental Handicap: Transitions in the Lives of People with Mental Handicaps*. London: Jessica Kingsley, pp. 22–37.

Bolton, R. (1979) *People Skills*. Englewood Cliffs, NJ: Prentice-Hall.

Bower, S.A. and Bower, G.H. (1976) *Asserting Yourself*. Reading, MA: Addison-Wesley.

Brammer, L.M. (1988) *The Helping Relationship* (4th edn). Englewood Cliffs, NJ: Prentice-Hall.

Broadfoot, P. (1989) 'Reporting to parents on student achievement: the UK experience.' Working Paper No. 2/89 (October) Bristol University.

Bronfenbrenner, U. (1976) 'Is early intervention effective?' In Clarke, A.M. and Clarke, A.D.B. (eds) *Early Experience: Myth and Evidence*. London: Open Books, pp. 247–56.

Bronfenbrenner, U. (1979) *The Ecology of Human Development*. Cambridge, MA: Harvard University Press.

Brotherson, M.J., Turnbull, A.P., Summers, J.A. and Turnbull, H.R. (1986) 'Fathers of disabled children'. In Robinson, B.E. and Barret, R.L. (eds) *The Developing Father*. New York: Guilford, pp. 193–217.

Brouillette, R., Thorburn, M. and Yamaguchi, K. (1993) 'Early childhood special education: an international perspective'. In Mittler, P., Brouillette, R. and Harris, D. *Special Needs Education: World Yearbook of Education 1993*. London: Kogan Page, pp. 175–84.

Bryans, T., Kidd, A. and Levey, M. (1985) 'The Kings Heath project'. In Topping and Wolfendale, op. cit., pp. 231–40.

Burgoyne, J. (1984) *Breaking Even: Divorce, Your Children and You*. Harmondsworth: Penguin.

Burton, L. (ed.) (1974) *The Care of the Child Facing Death*. London: Routledge & Kegan Paul.

Burton, L. (1975) *The Family Life of Sick Children*. London: Routledge & Kegan Paul.

Cattermole, J. and Robinson, N. (1985) Effective home/school communication – from the parents' perspective. *Phi Delta Kappan* **67** (2), 48–50.

Chilman, C.S., Nunnally, E.W. and Cox, F.M. (eds) (1988) *Chronic Illness and Disability*. Newbury Park, CA: Sage.

Chinn, P.C., Winn, J. and Walters, R.H. (1978) *Two Way Talking with Parents of Special Children*. St Louis: C.V. Mosby.

Collins, D., Tank, M. and Basith, A. (1993) *Concise Guide to Customs of Minority Ethnic Religions*. Aldershot: Ashgate.

Corey, G. (1990) *Theory and Practice of Group Counseling* (3rd edn). Pacific Grove, CA: Brooks/Cole.

Cox, K.M. and Desforges, M. (1987) *Divorce and the School*. London: Methuen.

Crnic, K.A. and Leconte, J.M. (1986) 'Understanding sibling needs and influences'. In Fewell and Vadasy, op. cit., pp. 75–98.

Cunningham, C. and Davis, H. (1985) *Working with Parents: Frameworks for Collaboration*. Milton Keynes: Open University Press.

Cunningham, C.C. and Jeffree, D.M. (1975) The organization and structure of workshops for parents of mentally handicapped children. *Bulletin of the British Psychological Society* **28**, 405–11.

Cyster, R., Clift, P.S. and Battle, S. (1979) *Parental Involvement in Primary Schools*. Windsor: NFER.

Davis, H. (1993) *Counselling Parents of Children with Chronic Illness or Disability*. Leicester: British Psychological Society.

Department for Education (DFE) (1993) *Reports on Pupils' Achievements*. London: DFE.

Department for Education (DFE) (1994) *Code of Practice on the Identification and Assessment of Special Educational Needs*. London: DFE.

Department of Education and Science (DES) (1967) *Children and Their Primary Schools* (Plowden Report). London: HMSO.

Department of Education and Science (DES) (1978) *Special Educational Needs* (Warnock Report). London: HMSO.

Dinkmeyer, D.C. and McKay, G.D. (1976) *Systematic Training for Effective Parenting*. Circle Pines, MN: American Guidance Service.

Dinkmeyer, D.C. and Muro, J.J. (1979) *Group Counselling: Theory and Practice* (2nd edn). Itasca, IL: Peacock.

Dyregrov, A. (1991) *Grief in Children: A Handbook for Adults*. London: Jessica Kingsley.

Egan, G. (1982) *The Skilled Helper* (2nd edn). Monterey, CA: Brooks/Cole.

Eiser, C. (1993) *Growing up with a Chronic Disease: The Impact on Children and Their Families*. London: Jessica Kingsley.

Elliott, J.A. and Hewison, J. (1994) Comprehension and interest in home reading. *British Journal of Educational Psychology* **64**, 203–20.

Featherstone, H. (1981) *A Difference in the Family*. Harmondsworth: Penguin.

Ferrari, M. (1984) Chronic illness: psychosocial effects on siblings – I. Chronically ill boys. *Journal of Child Psychology and Psychiatry* **25**, 459–76.

Fewell, R.R. and Vadasy, P.F. (eds) (1986) *Families of Handicapped Children*. Austin, TX: PRO-ED.

Fullwood, D. & Cronin, P. (1986) *Facing the Crowd: Managing Other People's Insensitivities to Your Disabled Child*. Melbourne: Royal Victorian Institute for the Blind.

Furneaux, B. (1988) *Special Parents*. Milton Keynes: Open University Press.

Gallagher, J.J., Beckman, P. and Cross, A.H. (1983) Families of handicapped children: sources of stress and its amelioration. *Exceptional Children* **50**, 10–19.

Gargiulo, R.M. (1985) *Working with Parents of Exceptional Children: A Guide for Professionals*. Boston: Houghton Mifflin.

Gath, A. (1977) The impact of an abnormal child upon the parents. *British Journal of Psychiatry* **130**, 405–10.

Gath, A. and Gumley, D. (1984) Down's syndrome and the family: follow-up of children first seen in infancy. *Developmental Medicine & Child Neurology* **26**, 500–8.

George, J.D. (1988) Therapeutic intervention for grandparents and extended family of children with developmental delays. *Mental Retardation* **26** (6), 369–75.

Gitterman, A. and Shulman, L. (eds) (1986) *Mutual Aid Groups and the Life Cycle*. Itasca, IL: Peacock.

Glynn, T. (1985) Remedial reading at home. In Topping and Wolfendale, op. cit., pp. 181–8.

Glynn, T. and Glynn, V. (1986) Shared reading by Cambodian mothers and children learning English as a second language: reciprocal gains. *The Exceptional Child* **33** (3), 159–72.

Glynn, T., McNaughton, S.S., Robinson, V. and Quinn, M. (1979) *Remedial Reading at Home: Helping You to Help Your Child*. Wellington, NZ: New Zealand Council for Educational Research.

Gordon, T. (1970) *Parent Effectiveness Training*. New York: Wyden.

Graziano, A.M. and Diament, D.M. (1992) Parent behavioral training: an examination of the paradigm. *Behavior Modification* **16** (1), 3–38.

Greening, N. and Spenceley, J. (1984) Paired Reading made easy. *Psychology* **11** (2), 10–14.

Griffiths, A. and Hamilton, D. (1984) *Parent, Teacher, Child: Working Together in Children's Learning*. London: Methuen.

Grossman, F. (1972) *Brothers and Sisters of Retarded Children*. Syracuse, NY: Syracuse University Press.

Hallahan, D.P. and Kauffman, J.K. (1991) *Exceptional Children: Introduction to Special Education* (5th edn). Englewood Cliffs, NJ: Prentice Hall.

Hannon, P. (1987) A study of the effects of parental involvement in the teaching of reading on children's reading test performance. *British Journal of Educational Psychology* **57** (1), 56–72.

Hannon, P., Jackson, A. and Page, B. (1985) 'Implementation and take-up of a project to involve parents in the teaching of reading'. In Topping and Wolfendale, op. cit., pp. 54–64.

Harding, J. and Pike, G. (1988) *Parental Involvement in Secondary Schools*. London: ILEA Learning Resources Branch.

Harris, T.A. (1969) *I'm O.K. – You're O.K.* New York: Harper & Row.

Hatch, S. and Hinton, T. (1986) *Self-Help in Practice*. Sheffield: Joint Unit for Social Services Research.

Hewison, J. (1985) 'Parental involvement and reading attainment: implications of research in Dagenham and Haringey'. In Topping and Wolfendale, op. cit., pp. 42–53.

Hodges, W.F. (1991) *Interventions for Children of Divorce* (2nd edn). New York Wiley.

Holland, S. and Ward, C. (1990) *Assertiveness: A Practical Approach*. Bicester: Winslow Press.

Hopmeyer, E. and Werk, A. (1993) A comparative study of four family bereavement groups. *Groupwork* **6** (2), pp. 107–21.

Hornby, G. (1980) Group counselling with parents of the intellectually handicapped. *Mental Handicap in New Zealand*, **5** (2), 3–14.

Hornby, G. (1982) Meeting the counselling and guidance needs of parents with intellectually handicapped children. *Mental Handicap in New Zealand* **6**, 8–27.

Hornby, G. (1987) 'Families with exceptional children'. In Mitchell, D.R. and Singh, N.N. (eds) *Exceptional Children in New Zealand*. Palmerston North, NZ: Dunmore Press, pp. 118–29.

Hornby, G. (1988) Launching Parent to Parent schemes. *British Journal of Special Education* **15** (2), 77–8.

Hornby, G. (1989) A model for parent participation. *British Journal of Special Education* **16** (4), 161–2.

Hornby, G. (1990) Training teachers to work with parents of children with special educational needs. *British Journal of In-Service Education* **16** (2), 116–18.

Hornby, G. (1992) Group parent training using reflective counselling and behavioural training procedures. *British Journal of Mental Subnormality* **38** (2), 79–86.

Hornby, G. (1994a) Effects of children with disabilities on fathers: a review and analysis of the literature. *International Journal of Disability, Development and Education* **41** (3), 171–84.

Hornby, G. (1994b) *Counselling in Child Disability*. London: Chapman & Hall.

Hornby, G. (1995a) Effects of children with Down syndrome on families: fathers' views. *Journal of Child and Family Studies* **4**, 103–17.

Hornby, G. (1995b) Effects on fathers of children with Down syndrome. *Journal of Child and Family Studies* (in press).

Hornby, G. and Ashworth, T. (1994) Grandparent support for families who have children with disabilities: a survey of parents. *Journal of Child and Family Studies* **3**, 403–12.

Hornby, G. and Murray, R. (1983) Group programmes for parents of children with various handicaps. *Child: Care, Health and Development* **9**, 185–98.

Hornby, G. and Murray, R. (1987) 'Preparation of professionals for special education'. In Mitchell, D.R. and Singh, N.N. (eds) *Exceptional Children in New Zealand*. Palmerston North, NZ: Dunmore Press, pp.197–211.

Hornby, G., Murray, R. and Davies, L. (1993) *Parent to Parent: Basic Helping/ Supporting Skills: Leader's Manual*. Auckland, NZ: Auckland College of Education.

Hornby, G., Murray, R. and Jones, R. (1987) Establishing a Parent to Parent service. *Child: Care, Health and Development* **13**, 277–88.

Hornby, G. and Peshawaria, R.P. (1991) Teaching counselling skills for working with parents of mentally handicapped children in a developing country. *International Journal of Special Education* **6** (2), 231–6.

Hornby, G. and Singh, N.N. (1982) Reflective group counselling for parents of mentally retarded children. *British Journal of Mental Subnormality* **28**, 71–6.

Hornby, G. and Singh, N.N. (1983) Group training for parents of mentally retarded children: a review and methodological analysis. *Child: Care, Health and Development* **9** (3), 199–213.

Hornby, G. and Singh, N.N. (1984) Behavioural group training with parents of mentally retarded children. *Journal of Mental Deficiency Research* **28**, 43–52.

Hornby, G., Wickham, P. and Zielinski, A. (1991) Establishing competencies for training teachers of children with special educational needs. *European Journal of Special Needs Education* **6** (1), 30–6.

Howard, S. and Hollingsworth, A. (1985) Linking home and school in theory and practice. *Journal of Community Education* **4** (3), 12–18.

Hughes, N. and Carpenter, B. (1991) 'Annual reviews: an active partnership'. In Ashdown, R., Carpenter, B. and Bovair, K. (eds) *The Curriculum Challenge*. London: Falmer Press, pp. 209–22.

Johnson, D.W. and Johnson, R.T. (1987) *Learning Together and Alone* (2nd edn). Englewood Cliffs, NJ: Prentice-Hall.

Jowett, S., Baginsky, M. and MacNeil, M.M. (1991) *Building Bridges: Parental Involvement in Schools*. Windsor: NFER-Nelson.

Kelley, M.L. (1990) *School–Home Notes: Promoting Children's Classroom Success*. New York: Guilford.

Klein, S.D. and Schleifer, M.J. (eds) (1993) *It Isn't Fair! Siblings of Children with Disabilities*. Westport, CT: Bergin & Garvey.

Kroth, R.L. (1985) *Communicating with Parents of Exceptional Children* (2nd edn). Denver, CO: Love.

Kübler-Ross, E. (1969) *On Death and Dying*. New York: Macmillan.

Lamb, M.E. (1983) 'Fathers of exceptional children'. In Seligman, M. (ed.) *The Family with a Handicapped Child*. New York: Grune & Stratton, pp. 125–46.

Lansdown, R. (1980) *More than Sympathy: The Everyday Needs of Sick and Handicapped Children and their Families*. London: Tavistock.

Lombana, J.H. (1983) *Home–School Partnerships: Guidelines and Strategies for Educators*. New York: Grune & Stratton.

Lonsdale, G. (1978) Family life with a handicapped child: the parents speak. *Child: Care, Health and Development*, **4**, 99–120.

McAndrew, I. (1976) Children with a handicap and their families. *Child: Care, Health and Development* **2**, 213–37.

McConachie, H. (1986) *Parents and Young Mentally Handicapped Children: A Review of Research Issues*. London: Croom Helm.

McConkey, R. (1985) *Working with Parents: A Practical Guide for Teachers and Therapists*. London: Croom Helm.

McConkey, R. and McCormack, C. (1983) *Breaking Barriers*. London: Souvenir Press.

McNaughton, S.S., Glynn, T. and Robinson, V. (1987) *Pause, Prompt and Praise: Effective Tutoring for Remedial Reading* (book and videotape). Birmingham: Positive Products.

Manthei, M. (1981) *Positively Me: A Guide to Assertive Behaviour* (rev. edn). Auckland, NZ; Methuen.

Max, L. (1985) 'Parents' views of provisions, services and research'. In Singh, N.N. and Wilton, K.M. (eds) *Mental Retardation in New Zealand*. Christchurch, NZ: Whitcoulls, pp. 250–62.

Merrett, F. (1988) Peer tutoring of reading using the 'Pause, Prompt and Praise' techniques. *Educational and Child Psychology*, **5** (4), pp. 17–23.

Meyer, D.J. (1986a) 'Fathers of handicapped children'. In Fewell and Vadasy, op. cit., pp. 35–73.

Meyer, D.J. (1986b) 'Fathers of children with mental handicaps'. In Lamb, M.E. (ed.) *The Father's Role: Applied Perspectives*. New York: Wiley, pp. 227–54.

Meyer, D.J., Vadasy, P.F. and Fewell, R.R. (1985a) *Living with a Brother or Sister with Special Needs*. Seattle: University of Washington Press.

Meyer, D.J., Vadasy, P.F. and Fewell, R.R. (1985b) *Sibshops: A Handbook for Implementing Workshops for Siblings of Children with Special Needs*. Seattle: University of Washington Press.

Meyer, D.J., Vadasy, P.F., Fewell, R.R. and Schell, G.C. (1985) *A Handbook for the Fathers Program*. Seattle: University of Washington Press.

Mink, I.T. and Nihira, K. (1987) Direction of effects: family life styles and behaviour of TMR children. *American Journal of Mental Deficiency* **92** (1), 57–64.

Minnes, P.M. (1988) 'Family stress associated with a developmentally handicapped child'. In Bray, N.W. (ed.) *International Review of Research in Mental Retardation* 15. London: Academic Press, pp. 195–226.

Mitchell, A. (1982) *When Parents Split Up: Divorce Explained to Young People*. Edinburgh: MacDonald.

Mitchell, D.R. (1985) 'Guidance needs and counselling of parents of persons with intellectual handicaps'. In Singh, N.N. and Wilton, K.M. (eds) *Mental Retardation in New Zealand*. Christchurch, NZ: Whitcoulls, pp. 136–56.

Mittler, P. (undated) 'Checklist of questions on home–school links'. Unpublished manuscript. University of Manchester.

Mittler, P. and McConachie, H. (1983) *Parents, Professionals and Mentally Handicapped Children*. London: Croom Helm.

Morgan, A. (1993) Training responses to the changing role of parents. *Community Education Network* **13** (6), 2–3.

Morgan, S.R. (1985) *Children in Crisis: A Team Approach in the Schools*. London: Taylor & Francis.

Moses, R., Kamii, M., Swap, S. and Howard, J. (1989) The algebra project: organizing in the spirit of Ella. *Harvard Educational Review* **59** (4), 423–43.

Mulder, V. (1994) Words can make it better. *Times Educational Supplement* (Review Section) (25 March), 5.

Murphy, M.A. (1982) The family with a handicapped child: a review of the literature. *Developmental and Behavioral Pediatrics* **3**, 73–82.

Myers, J.E. and Perrin, N. (1993) Grandparents affected by parental divorce: a population at risk? *Journal of Counseling and Development* **72** (1), 62–6.

Newsome, E. and Hipgrave, T. (1982) *Getting Through to Your Handicapped Child*. Cambridge: Cambridge University Press.

Olshansky, S. (1962) Chronic sorrow: a response to having a mentally defective child. *Social Casework* **43**, 190–3.

Ordal, C.C. (1984) Death as seen in books suitable for young children. *Omega: Journal of Death and Dying* **14**, 249–77.

Patterson, G.R. (1975) *Families: Applications of Social Learning to Family Life* (rev. edn). Champaign, IL: Research Press.

Philip, M. and Duckworth, D. (1982) *Children with Disabilities and Their Families: A Review of the Research*. Windsor: NFER-Nelson.

Pieper, E. (1976) Grandparents can help. *The Exceptional Parent* (7–9 April).

Powell, T.H. and Ogle, P.A. (1992) *Brothers and Sisters: A Special Part of Exceptional Families* (2nd edn). Baltimore: Paul H. Brookes.

Pugh, G. and De'Ath, E. (1984) *The Needs of Parents: Practice and Policy in Parent Education*. London: Macmillan.

Rando, T.A. (1988) *How to Go On Living When Someone You Love Dies*. Boston, MA: Lexingham.

Rinn, R.C. and Markle, A. (1977) Parent Effectiveness Training: a review. *Psychological Reports* **41**, 95–109.

Roesel, R. and Lawlis, G.F. (1983) Divorce in families of genetically handicapped/mentally retarded individuals. *American Journal of Family Therapy* **11** (1), 45–50.

Rogers, C.R. (1980) *A Way of Being*. Boston: Houghton Mifflin.

Romanoff, B.D. (1993) When a child dies: special considerations for providing mental health counseling for bereaved parents. *Journal of Mental Health Counseling* **15** (4), 384–93.

Roos, P. (1978) 'Parents of mentally retarded children: misunderstood and mistreated'. In Turnbull, H.R. and Turnbull, A.P. (eds) *Parents Speak Out*. Columbus, OH: Charles E. Merrill, pp. 245–57.

Rose, S.D. (1977) *Group Therapy: A Behavioural Approach*. Englewood Cliffs, NJ: Prentice-Hall.

Rutter, M. (1966) *Children of Sick Parents*. London: Oxford University Press.

Schiff, H.S. (1977) *The Bereaved Parent*. New York: Crown.

Schilling, R.F. (1988) 'Helping families with developmentally disabled members'. In Chilman, Nunnally and Cox, op. cit., pp. 171–92.

Scott, L. (1993) *Governors and Special Educational Needs*. London: London Advisory Centre for Education.

Seligman, M. (1979) *Strategies for Helping Parents of Exceptional Children: A Guide for Teachers*. New York: Free Press.

Seligman, M. (1990) Group approaches for parents of children with disabilities. In Seligman, M. and Marshak, L.E. (eds) *Group Psychotherapy: Interventions with Special Populations*. Boston: Allyn & Bacon.

Seligman, M. and Darling, R.B. (1989) *Ordinary Families: Special Children*. New York: Guilford.

Shearer, M.S. and Shearer, D.E. (1972) The Portage Project: a model for early childhood education. *Exceptional Children* **39** (3), 210–17.

Sicley, D. (1993) Effective methods of communication: practical interventions for classroom teachers. *Intervention in School and Clinic* **29** (2), 105–8.

Simeonsson, R.J. and McHale, S. (1981) Review: research on handicapped children: sibling relationships. *Child: Care, Health and Development* **7**, 153–71.

Simpson, R.L. (1990) *Conferencing Parents of Exceptional Children* (2nd edn). Austin, TX: PRO-ED.

Sonnek, I.M. (1986) 'Grandparents and the extended family of handicapped children'. In Fewell and Vadasy, op. cit., pp. 99–120.

Sonnenschien, P. (1984) 'Parents and professionals: an uneasy relationship'. In Henninger, M.L. and Nesselroad, E.M. (eds) *Working with Parents of Handicapped Children: A Book of Readings for School Personnel*. Lanham, MD: University Press of America, pp. 129–39.

Statham, J., MacKinnon, D. and Cathcart, H. (1989) *The Education Fact File*. London: Hodder & Stoughton.

Stewart, J.C. (1986) *Counseling Parents of Exceptional Children* (2nd edn). Columbus, OH: Merrill.

Stone, J. and Taylor, F. (1977) *A Handbook for Parents with a Handicapped Child*. London: Arrow.

Stone, L. (1993) Inspecting special: a new approach. *Special* (September), 33–7.

Sullivan, M. (1988) *Parents and Schools*. Leamington Spa: Scholastic Publications.

Swap, S.M. (1993) *Developing Home–School Partnerships*. New York: Teachers College Press.

Tavormina, J.B. (1974) Basic models of parent counselling: a review. *Psychological Bulletin* **8** (11), 827–35.

Tavormina, J.B. (1975) Relative effectiveness of behavioral and reflective group counselling with parents of mentally retarded children. *Journal of Consulting and Clinical Psychology* **43**, 22–31.

Tavormina, J.B., Hampson, R.B. and Luscomb, R. (1976) Participant evaluations of the effectiveness of their parent counselling groups. *Mental Retardation* **14**, 8–9.

Tew, B.J., Payne, E.H. and Lawrence, K.M. (1974) Must a family with a handicapped child be a handicapped family? *Developmental Medicine and Child Neurology* **16**, 95–8.

Thornton, C. and Krajewski, J. (1993) Death education for teachers. *Intervention in School and Clinic* **29** (1), 31–5.

Tizard, B., Mortimore, J. and Burchell, B. (1981) *Involving Parents in Nursery and Infant Schools*. London: Grant McIntyre.

Tizard, J., Schofield, W. and Hewison, J. (1982) Collaboration between teachers and parents in assisting children's reading. *British Journal of Educational Psychology* **52** (1), 1–11.

Topping, K. (1985) 'Review and prospect'. In Topping and Wolfendale, op. cit., pp. 287–96.

Topping, K. (1986) *Parents as Educators: Training Parents to Teach Their Children*. London: Croom Helm.

Topping, K. and Lindsay, G.A. (1992) Paired reading: a review of the literature. *Research Papers in Education* **7** (3), 199–246.

Topping, K. and Wolfendale, S. (eds) (1985) *Parental Involvement in Children's Reading*. London: Croom Helm.

Townsend, S. (1982) *The Growing Pains of Adrian Mole*. London: Methuen.

Trotzer, J.P. (1977) *The Counselor and the Group: Integrating Theory, Training and Practice*. Monterey, CA: Brooks/Cole.

Turnbull, A.P. and Turnbull, H.R. (1986) *Families, Professionals and Exceptionality*. Columbus, OH: Merrill.

Vadasy, P.F., Fewell, R.R., and Meyer, D.J. (1986) Grandparents of children with special needs: insights into their experiences and concerns. *Journal of the Division for Early Childhood* **10** (1), 36–44.

Vadasy, P.F., Fewell, R.R., Meyer, D.J. and Greenberg, M.T. (1985) Supporting fathers of handicapped young children: preliminary findings of program effects. *Analysis and Intervention in Developmental Disabilities* **5**, 151–63.

Visher, E. and Visher, J. (1982) *How to Win as a Stepfamily*. Chicago: Contemporary Books.

Wadsworth, D.E., Knight, D. and Balser, V. (1993) Children who are medically fragile or technology dependent: guidelines. *Intervention in School and Clinic* **29** (2), 102–14.

Walker, C.E., Bonner, B.L. and Kaufman, K.L. (1988) *The Physically and Sexually Abused Child: Evaluation and Treatment*. New York: Pergamon.

Webster, E.J. (1977) *Counselling Parents of Handicapped Children*. New York: Grune & Stratton.

White, M. and Cameron, R.J. (eds) (1988) *Portage: Progress, Problems and Possibilities*. Windsor: NFER-Nelson.

Wikler, L. (1981) Chronic stresses in families of mentally retarded children. *Family Relations* **30**, 281–8.

Wikler, L. (1986) Periodic stresses of families of older mentally retarded children: an exploratory study. *American Journal of Mental Deficiency* **90**, 703–6.

Wikler, L., Wasow, M. and Hatfield, E. (1981) Chronic sorrow revisited. *American Journal of Orthopsychiatry* **51**, 63–70.

Wikler, L., Wasow, M. and Hatfield, E. (1983) Seeking strengths in families of developmentally delayed children. *Social Work* **28**, 313–15.

Williamson, D.L. (1982) *Group Power: How to Develop, Lead, and Help Groups Achieve Goals*. Englewood Cliffs, NJ: Prentice-Hall.

Wolfendale, S. (1983) *Parental Participation in the Education and Development of Children*. London: Gordon & Breach.

Wolfendale, S. (ed.) (1989) *Parental Involvement: Developing Networks Between School, Home and Community*. London: Cassell.

Wolfendale, S. (1992) *Empowering Parents and Teachers*. London: Cassell.

Wolfendale, S. (ed.) (1993) *Assessing Special Educational Needs*. London: Cassell.

Worden, J.W. (1991) *Grief Counselling and Grief Therapy* (2nd edn). London: Routledge.

Yalom, I.D. (1985) *The Theory and Practice of Group Psychotherapy* (3rd edn). New York: Basic Books.

Young, S.J. (1991) 'The involvement of parents in the education of their physically disabled child'. Unpublished MEd thesis, University of Hull.

Name Index

Adler, A. 150
Allan, J. 75, 84, 100
Arora, T. 138
Ashworth, T. 59
Atkeson, K.M. 125
Atkin, J. 22, 25
Attwood, T. 152

Babcock, D.E. 151
Bamford, J. 138
Bastiani, J. 22, 23, 27, 114, 118
Batshaw, M.L. 8
Bell, R.Q. 43
Berger, M. 44
Berkowitz, B.P. 131
Berne, E. 151
Berrueta-Clement, J. 127, 128, 129
Bertoia, J. 75
Bicknell, J. 37
Bolton, R. 88, 94, 99
Bower, G.H. 98
Bower, S.A. 98
Brammer, L.M. 88
Broadfoot, P. 140
Bronfenbrenner, U. 45, 128
Brotherson, M.J. 57
Brouillette, R. 130
Bryans, T. 136
Burgoyne, J. 86
Burton, L. 63

Cameron, R.J. 28, 130

Carpenter, B. 142
Cattermole, J. 106
Chilman, C.S. 44
Chinn, P.C. 121
Collins, D. 9
Corey, G. 148
Cox, K.M. 79, 82, 83
Crnic, K.A. 59
Cronin, P. 8
Cunningham, C.C. 18, 21, 22, 152
Cyster, R. 22, 28

Darling, R. 58
Davis, H. 18, 21, 22, 63
De'Ath, E. 22, 28
Desforges, M. 79, 82, 83
Diament, D.M. 131, 132, 152
Dinkmeyer, D.C. 145, 146, 150
Duckworth, D. 8, 58
Dyregrov, A. 78

Egan, G. 100
Eiser, C. 62, 63
Elliott, J.A. 136

Featherstone, H. 26, 41, 57, 61
Ferrari, M. 59
Fewell, R.R. 56
Forehand, R. 125
Foster, M. 44
Fullwood, D. 8

Furneaux, B. 8

Gallagher, J.J. 58
Gargiulo, R.M. 22, 37
Gath, A. 57
George, J.D. 59
Gitterman, A. 159
Glynn, T. 126, 136, 137
Glynn, V. 136
Gordon, T. 91, 92, 149
Graziano, A.M. 131, 132, 152
Greening, N. 135
Griffiths, A. 22, 25
Grossman, F. 59

Hallahan, D.P. 8
Hamilton, D. 22, 25
Hannon, P. 133, 134
Harding, J. 22, 27
Harris, T.A. 151
Hatch, S. 156
Hewison, J. 133, 136
Hinton, T. 156
Hipgrave, T. 132
Hodges, W.F. 80, 83
Holland, S. 95
Hollingsworth, A. 28
Hopmeyer, E. 79
Hornby, G. 23, 29, 37, 57, 59, 94,
      100, 103, 144, 152, 153, 155,
      156, 157, 162
Howard, S. 28
Hughes, N. 142

Jeffree, D. 152
Johnson, D.W. 65
Johnson, R.T. 65
Jowett, S. 22

Kauffman, J.K. 8
Keepers, T.D. 151
Kelley, M.L. 125

Klein, S.D. 58
Krajewski, J. 72
Kroth, R.L. 22, 23, 26, 95, 114, 119,
      120, 123, 145
Kübler-Ross, E. 37

Lamb, M.E. 56
Lansdown, R. 8, 62
Lawlis, G.F. 57
Leconte, K.A. 59
Lindsay, G. 136
Lombana, J.H. 22, 23
Lonsdale, G. 57

McAndrew, I. 58
McConachie, H. 21, 56
McConkey, R. 8, 22, 28, 155
McCormack, C. 8
McHale, S. 58
McKay, G.D. 150
McNaughton, S.S. 137
Manthei, M. 97
Markle, A. 150
Max, L. 41
Merrett, F. 137
Meyer, D.J. 56, 58, 158
Mink, I.T. 43
Minnes, P.M. 56, 57
Mitchell, D.R. 42, 86
Mittler, P. 21, 30
Morgan, A. 12
Morgan, S.R. 8, 21, 66, 68, 69, 70,
      71, 72, 73, 74, 80, 81, 82, 83
Moses, R. 127
Mulder, V. 78
Muro, J.J. 145, 146
Murphy, M.A. 58
Murray, R. 29, 144, 153, 162
Myers, J.E. 80

Nairne, J. 84, 100
Newsome, E. 132

Nihira, K. 43

Ogle, P.A. 58
Olshansky, S. 41
Ordal, C.C. 78

Patterson, G.R. 132
Perrin, N. 80
Peshawaria, R. 103
Philip, M. 8, 58
Pieper, E. 59
Pike, G. 22, 27
Powell, T.H. 58
Pugh, G. 22, 28

Rando, T.A. 78
Rinn, R.C. 150
Robinson, N. 106
Roesel, R. 57
Rogers, C.R. 7
Romanoff, B.D. 70
Roos, P. 6, 19, 41, 42
Rose, S.D. 146
Rutter, M. 66

Schiff, H.S. 78
Schilling, R.F. 159
Schleifer, M.J. 58
Scott, L. 12
Seligman, M. 9, 22, 25, 37, 58, 87, 110, 146
Shearer, D.E. 129
Shearer, M.S. 129
Shulman, L. 159
Sicley, D. 116
Simeonsson, R.J. 58
Simpson, R.L. 22, 28, 119, 121, 123
Singh, N.N. 152
Sonnek, I.M. 59, 158
Sonnenschien, P. 4
Spenceley, J. 135
Statham, J. 9

Stewart, J.C. 22
Stone, J. 8, 60
Stone, L. 11
Sullivan, M. 22, 26
Swap, S.M. 106, 107, 119, 127

Tavormina, J.B. 152
Taylor, F. 8, 60
Tew, B.J. 57
Thornton, C. 72
Tizard, B. 22
Tizard, J. 127, 133
Topping, K. 14, 19, 22, 25, 28, 131, 133, 135, 136, 138
Townsend, S. 86
Trotzer, J.P. 147, 148
Turnbull, A.P. 4, 9, 87, 105, 112, 113, 116, 117, 119, 123
Turnbull, H.R. 4, 9, 87, 105, 112, 113, 116, 117, 119, 123

Vadasy, P.F. 56, 158
Visher, E. 86
Visher, J. 86

Wadsworth, D.E. 64
Walker, C.E. 21
Ward, C. 95
Webster, E.J. 6
Werk, A. 79
White, M. 28, 130
Wikler, L. 6, 41
Williamson, D.L. 148
Wolfendale, S. 9, 15, 22, 23, 133, 135, 138, 139, 140, 141
Worden, J.W. 35, 40, 74, 75

Yalom, I.D. 145
Young, S.J. 105, 109

Subject Index

Acceptance 39
Action skills 147
Active listening 92
Actualizing loss 75
Adaptation to a significant loss 37
Advocacy groups 159
Aggression, dealing with 95–6
Aloneness 41
Anger 38
Approaches to parent involvement
  consumer model 20
  expert model 18
  partnership model 20
  transplant model 19
Assertion skills 93–100
Assertiveness
  muscle levels 94
  physical 94
  vocal 94
Assessments
  facilitating parental involvement
    139–42
  pro formas for parents 141–2
  what parents can contribute
    140–1
  what parents want 139–40
Attendance, facilitation of 107
Attentive silence 90
Attentiveness 88
Attitudes

needed to work effectively with
    parents 7
  of teachers towards parents 4–7

Behavioural group training 151–2
Bereaved children, guidelines for
    teachers 77
Brainstorming 102

Children coping with bereavement
    66–8
Children with disabilities 55–61
Children with medical conditions
    61–6
Clients, parents as 14
Co–educators, parents as 14
Collaboration, between parents
    and teachers 25, 31
Coming to terms, with a child's
    special needs 36
Communication, between parents
    and teachers 27, 32
Communication blocks 91
Communication of assessment and
    review results 60
Constructive feedback, giving 98
Consultants, parents as 15
Contingency plans 65
Continuum of reactions 37–41
Counselling children 84
Counselling model 100–1
Counselling parents 79, 84

Counselling skills 100–3
Criticism, responding to 94–5

Death
  children's understanding of 73
  of a parent 68
  of a sibling 70
  of other significant people 71
Denial 38
DESC script 98–9
Detachment 39
Disillusionment 41

Early intervention projects 128–30
Ecological model 45
Education, of parents 33
Education Acts, parental rights
  9–11
Effectiveness of parental
  involvement 127–8
Effects on children of medical
  conditions 62–3
Effects on families of children with
  disabilities 56
Effects on families of medical
  conditions 63
Empathy, need to develop, 64
Exosystem 48
Experts, parents as 13
Expressing feelings about loss 75
Expressing implications 102
Eye contact 88

Family life, restrictions on 57
Family systems perspective 43
Fathers 56
Fathers' programmes 158
Fundraisers, parents as 13

Gala days 107
Goal setting 102
Governors, parents as 12
Grandparents 59

Grandparents' workshops 158
Grief
  coping styles 77
  defences 77
  individual differences 77
  typical reactions 77
Grief counselling 74
Grief in children 74
Group dynamics 148–9
Group leadership skills 146–8
Group work
  benefits 145–6
  costs 146
Guidance needed by parents of
  bereaved children 78

Handbooks, for parents 114
Helpers, parents as 13
High/Scope Project 128–9
Home visits 64, 108–11
  guidelines 110–11
Home–school behaviour
  programmes 125
Home–school diaries 115–17
Home–school maths programmes
  138
Home–school reading programmes
  126

Identifying themes 102
Individual education plans (IEP) 65
Inequality 42
Informal contacts 106–8
Information
  from parents 23, 31, 64
  needed by parents 60
Information giving 102
Insignificance 42
Interaction skills 147

Knowledge needed to work
  effectively with parents 8

Letters home 115
Liaison
  between parents and teachers
      27, 32
  with health care professionals 65
Linking family members 61
Listening skills 88–93
Loss of immortality 42

Macrosystem 50
Marital relationships 57
Meetings
  conducting 121
  organization 119
  parents' goals 118
  preparation by parents 120
  reviews of 122–3
  teachers' goals 118
Mesosystem 47
Microsystem 45
Model for parent involvement 22–9
Mothers 56

Newsletters 115
Note-taking 121
Notes home 115
Notifying parents 119

Open days 107
Open posture 89
Open questions 90
Outings 107

Paired reading 135–6
Paraphrasing 91
Parent behavioural training 131–3
Parent education 28
  comparative effectiveness 152
Parent education groups 149–52
Parent education workshops
  format 154–5
  organization 153–4

rationale 153
Parent Effectiveness Training (PET)
      149–50
Parent listening to children's
      reading 133–5
Parent preferences 105
Parent to Parent
  leaders 157
  organization 157
  rationale 155
  recruitment 156
  training 156
Parent–teacher meetings 117–23
Parental involvement in reading
      133–7
Parental separation
  books on 86
  children's coping 79–83
  effects on children 80
      at different ages 82
  effects on family 80
Passive listening 90
Past orientation 42
Pause, Prompt and Praise 136–7
Peer acceptance, facilitation of 65
Personal invitations 107
Philosophical beliefs and values,
      examination of 41
Phoning parents 112
Phoning teachers 111
Policy
  on parental separation 83
  parental contributions to 26, 30
Portage project 129–30
Problem-solving 99, 122
Progress reports 117

Rapport building 121
Reaction skills 147
Recipients of information, parents
      as 12

Recorded daily messages 113
Records, need for 84
Re-experiencing grief 41
Referring on 77, 79
Re-investing emotional energy 76
Reorganization 39
Requests
  making of 97–8
  refusals 96–7
Resource, parents as 25, 31
Reviewing skills 102
Reviews
  facilitating parental involvement
    139–42
  pro formas for parents 142
Rights of parents 9–11
Roles of parents in education 12

Sadness 39
School productions 107
Self-help groups 159
Self-listening 91
Shared reading 135
Shock 37
Sibling workshops 158
Siblings 58
Skills for action planning 102
Skills for listening 101
Skills for understanding 101
Skills needed to work effectively
  with parents 9
Stages of emotional reaction 37

Structuring 101, 121
Suggesting alternative
    interpretations 102
Suggesting new perspectives 102
Summarizing 102
Support 33
  availability of 65
  for children 84
  for grieving children 76
  for parents 29
  provision of 61
Systematic Training for Effective
    Parenting (STEP) 150–1

Tasks and challenges for parents
    42
Teacher training for working with
    parents 162
Telephone contacts 111–13
Telephone tree 113
Termination 122
Termination skills 103
Transactional Analysis parent
    education 151
Two-way communication 60, 64, 78

Vulnerability 42

Weekly folder 116
Written communication 113–17